LEADERSHIP
A to Z

LEADERSHIP
A to Z

A GUIDE FOR THE APPROPRIATELY AMBITIOUS

JAMES O'TOOLE

Jossey-Bass Publishers
San Francisco

Jossey-Bass books and products are available through most bookstores. To contact Jossey-Bass directly, call (888) 378-2537, fax to (800) 605-2665, or visit our website at www.josseybass.com.

Substantial discounts on bulk quantities of Jossey-Bass books are available to corporations, professional associations, and other organizations. For details and discount information, contact the special sales department at Jossey-Bass.

Manufactured in the United States of America. The text is printed on acid-free recycled paper containing a minimum of 10 percent postconsumer waste.

Interior design by Paula Goldstein

"Come to the Edge" from *Selected Poems* by Christopher Logue. Reprinted by permission of Faber and Faber Limited.
"Health Chief Vows 'Brutal' Shake-Up if Managers Resist Change" by Carl Ingram, copyright 1996, *Los Angeles Times*. Reprinted by permission.
"Larry Bird Almost Runs a Democracy" by G. Vecsey, copyright 1998 by the New York Times Co. Reprinted by permission.

Library of Congress Cataloging-in-Publication Data

O'Toole, James.
    Leadership A to Z: a guide for the appropriately ambitious / James O'Toole. — 1st ed.
      p. cm. — (Jossey-Bass business & management series)
    Includes bibliographical references.
    ISBN 0-7879-4658-3
    1. Leadership. 2. Decision making. 3. Executive ability. 4. Management. I. Title. II. Series.
    HD57.7 .O87 1999
    658.4'092—dc21
                                                                                    99-6416

first edition
HB Printing   10 9 8 7 6 5 4 3 2 1

To Marilyn

Contents

LEADERSHIP
A to Z

Memorandum on Appropriate Ambition

To: The Reader
From: The Author
Subject: The Appropriate Ambitions of a Leader

The purpose of this book is to identify clearly what leaders need to do in order to create high-performing, self-renewing organizations. While most leadership books focus on who leaders *are* (their character, personality, style, and charisma), the accent here is on what leaders *do*. The shift in emphasis has a practical intent: although it is possible for you to learn from what others do, it is highly unlikely that you can become someone you aren't.

In fact, I believe only one inherent character trait is essential for effective leadership, and that is ambition. Obviously, you can't "learn to do" ambition, but I'm assuming you already have that trait or you wouldn't have bought this book! Nonetheless, it is perfectly understandable if you felt a hint of ambivalence about the "A" word on the cover when you picked it up at the bookstore. After all, you probably don't think of yourself as ambitious. Relax. Even the saintly Mohandas K. Gandhi had ambition. When asked why he had abandoned a successful law career (and a well-cushioned lifestyle) to pursue a risky, self-sacrificing career of political leadership, the Mahatma unhesitatingly replied with that single, stark, and appropriate word "Ambition!"

Granted, it is not necessarily an attractive personal trait, that desire for power, distinction, and public approval—overtly ambitious politicians and business leaders earn society's opprobrium, if not its well-deserved contempt. Julius Caesar, after all, was assassinated because, Antony states in his elegy, "Brutus says he was ambitious; / And Brutus is an honorable man."

Nonetheless, Gandhi chose exactly the right word to describe the force that compelled him to risk all—even his life—in the pursuit of a worthy goal. By his early forties, he had come to feel terror at the prospect of living to old age in conventional comfort. He trembled when he imagined himself on his deathbed uttering the most tragic of all last words: "I *could have* done much more with my life."

"Could have," "should have," "might have"—Gandhi rejected that sorry mantra. He was not going to die knowing he *could* have brought independence to India. Instead, he eagerly embraced the challenge of leadership. But his ambition was not strictly personal. He had high aspirations for his *country*: he was convinced that India could overcome its negative sense of economic, cultural, and political dependence on Britain and then become a self-sufficient, self-confident, and self-governing member of the community of sovereign nations. And he was willing to devote the entirety of his life to the realization of that ambition, even though at the beginning of his quest most Indians were unwilling to take up the challenge. But he would energize them, give them hope, and show them that, indeed, their deepest aspirations were realizable! For the next forty years, he focused nearly all his energies on the single goal of Indian independence. (Similarly, Julius Caesar is exonerated later, in Antony's oration, when Antony points out that everything Caesar did he did not for himself but for Rome: "he hath left you all his walks, / His private arbors and new-planted orchards, / On this side Tiber.")

Of course, not many leaders are as admirable in their behavior, as noble in their goals, or as successful in the practice of their craft as was Gandhi. Yet, all leaders are driven by that same overwhelming motivation called ambition. All effective leaders have the compelling desire to help their own nation, company, or organization achieve its highest potential. Moreover, they all are willing to put themselves on the line in order to achieve that end.

Jack Welch is the quintessential business example of ambitious leadership. Most CEOs would have been satisfied with General Electric's 1981 level of performance: its profits were high, it had blue-chip standing on Wall Street, and it was one of the country's most-respected corporations. But when Welch assumed leadership of the company that year, he wanted something more for GE: he wanted to make it the world's most competitive company.

Welch's motivation and behavior were far from Gandhian—let's have no illusions on that score—but he manifested the essential leadership trait of ambition, which clearly distinguished him from the host of more timid (and ultimately less successful) CEOs who directed the fortunes of corporate America in the eighties. Not only did Welch want true greatness for GE, but he was also committed personally to do all that was necessary to realize the company's full potential. That is appropriate ambition.

The Welches of the world realize that at any given time almost all organizations are seriously underperforming. Few companies come anywhere near achieving their potential, whether that is measured by profits, growth, market share, product quality, innovation, customer service, or employee development. Worse, most

CEOs—and other individuals in positions of titular authority in the public and private sectors—either are satisfied with the status quo or are fearful of assuming the personal risk of attempting to transform their organizations in order to achieve greatness. In sharp distinction are those few individuals who have high ambition for themselves and for their organizations. Those who act on that ambition are called leaders.

Indeed, odds are you know that your company (or your division, government agency, or nonprofit organization) is significantly underperforming, and that's what motivated you to buy this book. And the reason I wrote it is to build on that healthy dissatisfaction with the status quo and, then, to urge you to change it! My hope is that you will take on the responsibility of leadership. Wherever you work and whatever the managerial level you occupy, you have the opportunity to make things better.

I can't promise you will succeed if you take up that challenge, but I can assure you of this much at least: there is no more rewarding task in business than to lead a transformation in which an organization's potential is realized—as there is no more dispiriting condition than to stand by passively on the sidelines in an underperforming institution. Hence, it's in your self-interest, and the interest of your organization, that you start to think of yourself as a leader—and to act accordingly.

Having said that, I'd be less than candid if I didn't acknowledge how difficult leadership is—indeed, it is the most difficult of all social tasks to do well. The first obstacles to success are the formidable ones of knowing what to do and how to do it. To help you clear those hurdles, I've distilled in these pages much of what has been learned about leadership since the late 1970s. My sources include

- Practical lessons that leaders have drawn from their own experiences

- Findings from research conducted by prominent scholars
- Results of a two-year project on "strategic leadership" conducted by the consulting firm Booz·Allen & Hamilton
- My own conclusions based on thirty years of closely observing many inspiring (and more than a few disastrously incompetent) leaders in the public and private sectors

The bad news is this: despite the considerable effort that has gone into the study of leadership, what is known with scientific certainty about the subject can be stored in a thimble. Worse, most research has been wasted on futile attempts to measure and classify the multitude of personality types and "styles" of leaders. That approach is doomed to failure simply because each leader is, in essence, different. And even worse, the psychological focus on individual traits obscures the fundamental fact that leadership isn't a solo act. What truly matters is an organization's overall leadership capacity throughout its ranks.

The efforts to discover the wellsprings of leadership would have been for naught if it hadn't been for an unorthodox tack pursued by many of the authors (the ones with the asterisks) cited as "resources" at the bottom of the alphabetical entries that form the text of this guidebook. Instead of asking who leaders *are,* these imaginative authors and scholars have asked, "What do leaders *do?*" Their analyses of the actions of successful leaders in politics, business, and the professions reveal a strong and persistent pattern of behavior—despite obvious differences of personality and style.

Perhaps the most significant thing that great leaders have in common is that they don't do a lot of unfocused things. Rather than running around doing what everyone else ought, in fact, to be doing, they focus productively on a small set of actions necessary to cascade leadership down, and throughout, their organizations.

The good news for you is this: what successful leaders *do* is both learnable and replicable. Although there's no way you can learn to be someone else, there's no reason why you can't learn to *do* what others have successfully done. And everyone who wants to be a leader today now has access to practical knowledge concerning what successful leaders do to create high-performing and self-renewing organizations. Likewise, important lessons based on the experiences of leaders who have helped followers achieve their potential, and who have developed other leaders, are now available for all to draw on—and apply in their own organizations.

In choosing the examples cited here, I have opted wherever possible to use familiar names instead of fresh (that is, obscure) ones. Because my purpose is *not* biography, I've tried to pick the most common, most noncontroversial, and clearest examples possible to focus the reader's attention on each lesson being illustrated. I did not want an essential lesson of leadership to be missed because the reader was questioning whether Madonna is, in fact, a good example of the issue under discussion!

For similar reasons, I've cited few young leaders. Experience shows that it is risky in the extreme to predicate important lessons on the examples of individuals in the midst of their careers—individuals whose behavior invariably will disappoint or embarrass those who prematurely anoint them as "great" men and women. Lincoln may be a "tired" example, but at least we won't be surprised by an article in tomorrow's paper about a grand jury indictment.

So, for your benefit and use, here's what leaders do from A to Z. As you see, I've organized the information alphabetically and cut it down into bite-sized chunks you can sample over coffee or between meetings. And although it makes sense to start at the beginning of the alphabet, feel free to dip in anywhere.

A

LEADERSHIP
A to Z

ABB's Benchstrength

If you can do something best by doing it yourself—sell a product, create a computer program, solve an equation, write a book—by definition that activity does *not* require leadership. The A-number-one fact of organizational life is that leadership is never a solo act. Leadership is always a social, or group, activity that involves getting other people to do the right things. That's why we should be careful to place more emphasis on *leadership* than on *the leader*. Although it is clearly necessary for any group to have a leader (or two) at its head, such a thin layer of talent at the top will be insufficient for long-term success. A single leader is almost always required to act as a prime mover of change; but, in addition, high-performing and self-renewing organizations need deep reservoirs of leadership *benchstrength*.

The greatest of leaders are, in fact, leaders of leaders. In the mode of Jesus Christ, they create disciples. In eminent organizations, such disciples are not, as the analogy might imply, dutiful worshipers of the leader—that is, yes-men and yes-women whose only function is to carry out the will of the boss. Instead, effective disciples are true leaders in their own right who think for themselves and act accordingly, all the while sharing the master leader's basic vision, values, and overall philosophy of leadership. Indeed, the apostles Peter and Paul were strong leaders who were capable of carrying on independently after the death of the founder of their movement.

Almost all the greatest secular leaders have been leaders of leaders. Even the American president who is most often portrayed as a loner, Thomas Jefferson, surrounded himself with a first-rate team of leaders—James Madison, Albert Gallatin, James Monroe, and, until Jefferson sent him off on his famous expedition, Meriwether Lewis. More recently, Martin Luther King, Jr. was the leader of Jesse Jackson, Andrew Young, Julian Bond, Maynard Jackson, Coretta Scott King, Ralph Abernathy, and many of the other most prominent African-American leaders of the last half of the twentieth century.

In business, ABB's retired CEO Percy Barnevik won his sparkling reputation by creating an environment in which effective leadership permeated the entire organization, from headquarters to business units. During his career at ABB, Barnevik's highest priority was to create virtual Percys at all levels. Significantly, his interest was not in producing doppelgängers or clones who would carry out his bidding mindlessly, but, instead, he set himself the task of creating a cadre of independent leaders who nonetheless shared his belief that the true measure of a leader is the ability to motivate others to accept the responsibility to lead.

When Barnevik was named CEO of the newly merged ABB in 1987, he faced a challenge common to all leaders: he knew what needed to be done, but he couldn't do it all by himself. In fact, for ABB to succeed he needed the active cooperation—and entrepreneurial initiative—of some 200,000 employees spread all over the globe in dozens of relatively independent businesses. (Fortunately, most leaders don't face challenges that are quite so daunting; nonetheless, all leaders do have to work through others who have their own values and agendas.)

Barnevik reasoned that the only way in which he could achieve ABB's objectives was, first, to create a critical mass of other leaders who shared his vision and, second, for *them* to lead the required changes by, in turn, creating yet more leaders who would then cascade the behavior required for success right down to the front line. He understood that he would need leaders at each level of the organization who were accountable for discovering what changes were needed at ABB and, then, for making the operating decisions required for those changes to occur in a timely and coherent fashion. If he could create the conditions under which other leaders would do the operational work of change, Barnevik himself would be free to concentrate on the three leadership tasks that *only he* could do:

- Establish the overall ABB vision, values, strategy, goals, and objectives
- Create the structure, conditions, and architecture in which others could effectively carry out their tasks
- Evaluate, and then reward, those leaders down the line who successfully motivated their followers to behave in ways consistent with the ABB vision

The last of these three tasks proved the most difficult. Barnevik found that he could readily establish strategies and structures, but the hard-slogging, time-consuming task of leadership consists of forcing the work of change down to appropriate levels—and then holding people accountable. Naturally, he held his people accountable for their performance and for meeting commitments. But, more important, he held them accountable for assuming the responsibilities of leadership. This is difficult in all organizations because most people do not want to be held accountable for making changes—or, for that matter, for any actions that have potentially negative consequences for other people or for the bottom line. It is a simple fact of life that most people don't want the responsibility of leadership.

You can't blame them (and "them is *us*," as Pogo would say). After all, experience teaches us that when we stick our necks out and assume leadership responsibility, we will either (a) be punished if things go wrong or (b) be second-guessed even if they go right!

To understand point (b), try to recall the first time you were given authority to do a job. Perhaps you were asked to clean out your neighbor's garage. The neighbor said, "Mary, you are now eleven and old enough to make this messy garage neat, orderly, spick-and-span. I'll be back at five o'clock to inspect your work." With youthful energy and enthusiasm, you busted your little keister to make the joint shine. As the hour of five approached, you proudly surveyed your work, expecting soon to win approval and praise (and perhaps even a bonus).

So what did your neighbor probably say? "Hey, I told you to tidy the place up, but I never said anything about hosing down the floor! You didn't throw away my old *Life* magazines, did you? Why did you hide my tools where I can't find them? And who gave you permission to paint that wall? . . . "

No wonder people resist taking responsibility! When leaders attempt to "empower" them, common sense tells them (us) that nobody is ever fully empowered. There are always limits to our authority and negative consequences if we exceed those limits. Hence, quite sensibly, we don't believe it when our superiors tell us that we have decision-making authority. "Yeah, sure," we think, "but the boss doesn't mean it" (and then we act—or, rather, fail to act—accordingly).

From day one as CEO of ABB, Barnevik recognized that the company's success depended on overcoming the natural resistance of managers to take the initiative and to be held accountable. He understood that before ABB people would put themselves on the line, they needed to know exactly how much authority they had. Because his managers needed to know the boundaries and the rules of the game, Barnevik began his first meeting as leader of ABB by offering the following guidelines, which he called General Principles of Management Behavior:

- To take action (and stick out one's neck) and do the right things is obviously the best.
- To take action and do the wrong things (within reason and a limited number of times) is second best.
- Not to take action (and lose opportunities) is the only nonacceptable behavior.

Still, people pushed back. (In the real world, leadership is not a fairy tale in which followers immediately do the right thing; instead, people always act in their own perceived self-interest.) Indeed, for almost the next two years, people at all levels in ABB continued to try to kick important decisions back up the line. The common refrain was, "Boss, this is a tough decision; you'll have to make it." After all, why would any reasonable person want to be held accountable for a decision that might turn out to be wrong, that might be unpopular with others, or, worse, might cause people to lose their jobs? *Hell no, let the boss decide!*

But Barnevik recognized that if he let his people get away with it, all decisions would end up back on his desk. If that happened, the changes needed at ABB wouldn't occur, he would be making decisions that others were more qualified to make (by virtue of their proximity to relevant information), and people at all levels would be passively standing around with no stake in making sure that decisions were implemented. Moreover, unless people learned to address tough, ambiguous questions and to make decisions with real consequences, they wouldn't learn to be leaders—and ABB would be in the untenable, unproductive, and survival-threatening position of having only one qualified leader.

Harvard's Christopher Bartlett tells an instructive story about how one of Barnevik's disciples, Ulf Gundemark, followed Barnevik's example and created leaders three levels down in ABB. Gundemark had given a team of managers authority and responsibility to make a major decision involving the rationalization of operations across several nations. (In other words, the consequences were great: someone stood to lose resources, staff, markets, and status—the very essence of power in organizations.)

Naturally, the team resisted making the decision. They appealed to Gundemark to decide. But, nope, he held firm, and sent them off to come to a conclusion themselves. Still, they came back again with the same story. "We can't do it! It's too hard. Ulf, you'll have to decide." Gundemark remained unmovable. He repeated that the decision was *theirs*. Time and again, the team tried to get off the hook, but Gundemark held firm, giving them a no-excuses, do-it-now deadline and then holding them accountable for making the tough decision. *What a leader!*

Give yourself the same test. If you delegated an important decision to the people who report to you, would you have the courage and persistence to hold their feet to the fire and make them decide? Would you force them to learn to be leaders even if they flattered you by arguing that your insight and experience were required to make the right decision? I suspect that few of us would pass the test. Indeed, the hardest leadership task is holding people accountable—insisting that they take responsibility to act, make decisions, and become leaders themselves.

In sum, all the highest performing companies not only have competent leaders at the top, they are infused with effective leadership at all levels. As the capacity for leadership cascades down the ranks of a corporation, there is a multiplying effect on the organization's capability to compete, to grow, and to renew itself. In the end, companies with deep leadership benchstrength are the strongest organizations because they are not dependent on the abilities of a single person, no matter how capable he or she may be.

Resource: *Christopher Bartlett, "ABB's Relays Business: Building and Managing a Global Matrix," Harvard Business School Case 9-394-016, 1993.

ABCs of Business Success

L eadership is elementary stuff. In the corporate world, it often comes down to focusing the efforts of followers on such basics of business success as (a) producing quality products, (b) listening to customers, and (c) motivating employees to do the right things. That's what Richard Teerlink did from the minute he took control of the handlebars at Harley-Davidson in 1989. Once CEO Teerlink had formed a cohesive leadership team, they immediately set about resuscitating the nearly defunct—but once storied—Harley brand by getting all employees to pay attention to the ABCs of success in the motorcycle business:

A. *Bikers demand high performance.* Hence, Teerlink's team introduced a world-class quality-control program.
B. *Bikers want the mystique of "easy-rider" freedom.* Hence, Teerlink's team introduced HOGs (Harley Owner Groups) with chapters all over the land. In order to continually monitor the pulse of customers—

and get fresh product and marketing ideas—Harley managers regularly attend HOG meetings.

C. *Success requires aligning employee behavior to the needs of customers.* Hence, Teerlink's team put all five thousand employees on incentive compensation, rewarding them for their ideas and efforts to improve A and B (the quality and mystique of Harley products).

That's what Teerlink's team did. It is also worth noting what they did *not* do:

X. They didn't lay off scores of workers and managers to demonstrate how tough they were.

Y. They didn't grandstand by entering into a high-profile merger, acquisition, or spin-off.

Z. They didn't lock themselves up in the executive suite with a passel of bean counters who didn't know a Harley from a unicycle.

In short, by creating conditions under which all Harley employees would focus their attention on making and marketing high-quality products, Teerlink and his team completely transformed the Harley culture—and made megabucks for long-term investors in the process. *That's* the essence of corporate leadership. The mystery is why so many CEOs ignore the ABCs, jump to the XYZs, and then wonder why they inevitably and invariably fail.

Apologia

It occurred to me more than once while writing this book that my timing wasn't exactly propitious. So I might as well deal with the bitter reality up front and in an early chapter: *Yes, indeed, everyone today is more than a little cynical about leaders and leadership.* And it isn't just the continuing barrage of revelations about philandering presidents, crooked Congressmembers, and lawbreaking mayors that has caused us to become jaded. In fact, we've learned that even the head of the once revered United Way has had his hand in the till!

Leadership already had a bad name in four-fifths of the world as the result of decades of misrule by dictators, authoritarians, and run-of-the-mill satraps. Who in Europe, Asia, Africa, or Latin America could find anything positive to say about leadership after having experienced the tyranny of a Hitler, Stalin, Mao, Idi Amin, or even a petty despot like Juan Perón? And in an age that has witnessed increasingly equal opportunity to disappoint, the likes of Indira Gandhi, Benazir Bhutto, Imelda Marcos, Eva Perón—and even the powerless Rigoberta Menchú and Queen Elizabeth II—

have done little to assuage our skepticism about the wisdom of the entire leadership endeavor.

In the United States, mercifully, we have been spared the ravages of murderous leadership. Yet, exposés have unearthed evidence that even those few leaders we so revere that we refer to them by monikers—FDR, Ike, JFK—had feet of clay.

Indeed, the more we followers learn about those who govern us— in the capitol, the statehouse, and city hall—the more we become convinced that leaders rather than followers benefit from the relationship. You don't have to be totally jaundiced to feel that all we get from our leaders on the left are corruption, self-indulgence, greed, and hypocrisy, while the contributions from leaders on the right are intolerance, incompetence, greed, and hypocrisy. Big difference!

The record in the private sector hasn't been quite so dispiriting. Yet, even there, it is easier to identify more Neros than heroes, more self-serving egotists than far-sighted innovators, and more bureaucrats than builders. At the bottom of the barrel, we've witnessed the grand-scale buffoonery of Bendix's William Agee, General Motor's Roger Smith, Continental's Frank Lorenzo, and RJR Nabisco's superclown, F. Ross Johnson. Finally, Al Dunlap compromised whatever public respect remained for corporate chief executives when he posed for a publicity shot in full Rambo regalia. (See **D**unlap, "Chainsaw" Al.)

In all, it's easy to understand why the promise of leadership no longer makes hearts beat with the prospect of pride and glory—and why a lot of smart people today are passing on the opportunity to stand up and lead.

Still . . .

Yet . . .

On the other hand . . .

Without ignoring the bad apples, the inescapable truth is that leadership is not only important but essential. It is a requirement in any situation in which members of a group disagree about where they should be heading or about what they should be doing. Without leaders to focus efforts toward a common objective, people will run off on their separate ways—and societies will not progress, and organizations will not achieve their aims. Leadership is also the most difficult of all social tasks—and that perhaps accounts for why there are many more examples of failed leaders than of great ones.

So what should we take from this? Yes, leadership *is* hard. It is also indispensable. And it is axiomatic that the more important the endeavor, the harder it is to accomplish. Because leadership is the most important single activity in an organization, should we then be surprised to discover that it is also the hardest? So spare the excuses, and get to work. Nobody said this was going to be easy!

And what about those bad apples? Yes, they are discouraging. The silver lining in the otherwise gloomy picture is that there are also many counterexamples of positive leadership—and the pages of this book are filled with the names of men and women who have led their nations and organizations in ways that have allowed followers to realize their needs. Of course, none of those leaders was, or is, perfect; and none has completely fulfilled the aspirations of followers. That, alas, is the way of the world. (See **P**erfection.)

B

LEADERSHIP
A to Z

Behavior
(the Measure of Leadership)

Question: How do you know whether there is effective leadership in an organization?

Answer: When behavior throughout the organization is consistent with the stated vision, mission, objectives, and aspirations.

Hence, a would-be leader must keep the following in mind: in the final reckoning, it is not who *you* are but what *they* do. (See Metrics II.)

Brownian Motivation
(Challenging, Stretching, and Other Nonviolent Ways to Overcome Resistance to Change)

L eaders bring out the best in their followers. First, leaders inspire followers by showing them how good they are capable of becoming, and then they help followers realize their elevated aspirations. That's what Tina Brown did in her six years at *The New Yorker*. Her official title at that venerable institution was "editor," but she defined her real job as *leading change:* "The assignment I had been handed was renewal. And renewal would mean change, . . . [and] the prospect of change was, of course, bound to provoke a measure of consternation."

In any organization, the source of consternation about change is, in a word, fear. We resist change because we are afraid we can't cope, can't do the new things that are being asked of us, and, thus, we fear we will fail. We resist taking the risky route of change because it almost always seems more prudent—safer—to keep doing what we know how to do. Why should we walk a tightrope and end up disappointing everyone, especially ourselves, when we fall off?

The job of the leader is to overcome that all-too-common lack of self-confidence and to convince followers that we are, in fact, far more capable than we give ourselves credit for being. "Come on," the leader challenges, "I know you can do it. I know we can do it!" Did the leader say *we?* That makes a difference, doesn't it? For if we're in this together, we can help each other. And the leader starts that process by showing us how, teaching us, and building a safety net to catch us if we should fall off the tightrope while learning to walk it.

That's what Tina Brown did. Of course, she did a lot of other things as well—some of them controversial—but what her followers credit her for most was her dedication to developing their capacity to change and to grow. Tina Brown understood that leaders don't change organizations, *they change people.*

She started by changing her own role and even changing herself in the process. Her two fabled predecessors, Harold Ross and William Shawn, had been editors in the old school—aloof bosses who ruled imperiously from lofty perches whence they issued fiats to their minions below. Brown easily could have assumed that traditional editorial persona. But she swore she wasn't going to be a curator of the magazine's dusty past; instead, she was going to be a leader of change. "Retreating behind the moat and closing the siege doors on the world was, I believed, a self-defeating way to champion *The New Yorker's* values," she says.

So she got into the trenches—and into the faces of her staff. She questioned their assumptions, challenged their premises, and made them clarify their thinking. Each day, every hour, she engaged her people, making them defend what they proposed in terms of *The New Yorker's* values. She engaged in an ongoing dialogue with her people and, in the process, constantly reframed and refined her vision and the purpose of the magazine's renewal. She defended tradition with one hand—the values and mission of *The New Yorker*—and encouraged radical change with the other— questioning the outmoded assumptions that were causing the institution to suffocate from self-inflicted fustiness. "But when I look back I realize how much the experience changed me, too," Brown says. "Each day I had to thrash out my ideas with people who understood—and cared fervently about—the magazine's essential character."

According to writer Hendrik Hertzberg, Brown viewed the task of leadership as "pumping energy and life" into an organization that "was drifting inexorably toward dotage." She broke more than one icon in the process. Hertzberg says, "Didn't Chairman Mao once say that a revolution is not a dinner party? Well, this one was, with dancing till dawn." Brown opened the doors to the inner sanctum that had been the privileged domain of Ross and Shawn, and she let everyone in. She involved them. She engaged them. She made them responsible.

Writer Nancy Franklin explains the extent of the change: "Before Tina Brown came to *The New Yorker,* in 1992, there was no such thing as an editorial meeting. Since the editor-in-chief made all the substantive decisions regarding nonfiction, or 'fact,' pieces, there was no need for the fact editors to get together with him as a group. All that changed in 1992: fact editors now had to make assignments, accept and reject pieces, get involved in the planning of special issues, lobby for writers, explain why a writer had missed a deadline, haggle over word counts. Overnight, our duck pond had been turned into a speed-skating track."

When Brown retired, writers and editors alike gave testimony to how this constant interchange caused them to rethink not only what *The New Yorker* stood for but also what their role was in the enterprise. In particular, she formed a coaching relationship in which she forcefully made staff members think through their assumptions, and, in the process, she stretched them when their premises were too safe and easy. When they brought her inchoate story ideas that they wrongly assumed were clear and insightful, she could see what it was they wanted to say, and she helped them to define it. Of course they resisted! And of course they resented being questioned, probed, and made to try new things.

Even if the writers and editors weren't located in New York, she wore them out with countless querying notes, memos, and faxes. In this way she developed an entire new generation of writers and editors, including Nancy Franklin, Alison Rose, Connie Bruck, Adam Gopnik, Anthony Lane, and her successor, David Remnick. In the end, she left *them* capable of leading *The New Yorker* without her.

And in the end they came to understand what she was doing. In hindsight, they were appreciative in the way one looks back gratefully to a high school math teacher who convinced us that—contrary to our considered assessment of our own capabilities—we could, indeed, learn trigonometry. Franklin explains what the stretching and challenging meant for her: "Over the years, I've learned that if Tina has an idea for me that horrifies me, that makes me go farther than I'm comfortable going, it's probably a good one."

Because Tina Brown never let her people get away with doing what they could safely do, they all grew. In the process, *The New Yorker* changed, and a new team is now poised to write a fresh chapter in its storied history.

The contemporary British poet Christopher Logue captures the essence of such leadership:

> Come to the edge.
> We might fall.
> Come to the edge.
> It's too high!
> COME TO THE EDGE!
> And they came
> and he pushed
> and they flew . . .

Resources: Tina Brown, "Something Old, Something New," *New Yorker,* July 27, 1998.

The Talk of the Town, *New Yorker,* August 3, 1998.

Christopher Logue, *New Numbers* (London: Jonathan Cape, 1970), p. 81. Quoted by permission of the author.

C

LEADERSHIP
A to Z

Cascading Leadership

O n the facing page, here's a graphic
representation of what leaders do in
high-performing, self-renewing organizations:

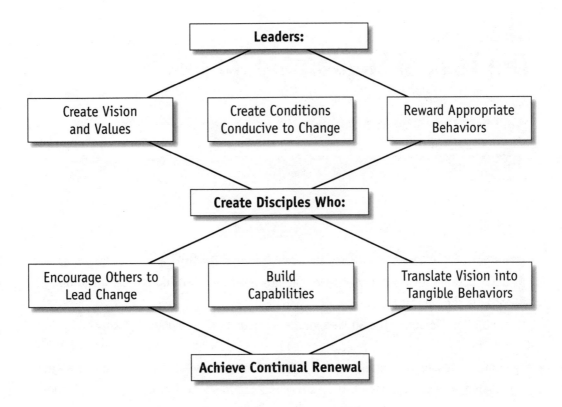

Leaders:

Create Vision and Values

Create Conditions Conducive to Change

Reward Appropriate Behaviors

Create Disciples Who:

Encourage Others to Lead Change

Build Capabilities

Translate Vision into Tangible Behaviors

Achieve Continual Renewal

Resource: *Booz·Allen & Hamilton, *Do You Know Your Company's S.L.Q.?* 1998.

Change:
The Task of Leadership (or Is It?)

In light of the activities of Percy Barnevik, Richard Teerlink, and Tina Brown, as described in previous chapters, we may now ask the following critical question: What is the central task of leadership?

To some, the answer will be as clear as the obvious fact that the world doesn't stand still: *change is the task of leadership*. After all, business executives and government officials who interpret their function as preserving the status quo are not remembered as leaders. Instead, they are called administrators or bureaucrats. Because change isn't an option in this hectic world, those who cannot embrace change should apply for a different position!

Yet, others will observe the behavior of great leaders and come to a different conclusion: *continuity, or coherence, is the task of leadership*. After all, what is more important than gaining the behavioral alignment of followers with an organization's values, principles, vision, and mission? Who could be called a great leader who didn't focus the activities of followers in a consistent, useful direction?

In fact, both these common observations are correct. To get away from thinking of them as contradictory, we need to reframe the traditional way we think about leadership. A more accurate way to understand the activities of Barnevik, Teerlink, Brown, and the other leaders you will meet in these pages is to keep in mind that true leadership has two primary, and equally important, dimensions: Alignment and Adaptability.

The first task of a leadership team is to create Alignment between its vision and the behavior of all the individuals in the organization. This means nothing less than creating coherence among all operating systems in a business—including planning, budgeting, measurement, and rewards. Well-aligned organizations succeed because all their efforts are focused toward a common end.

Unfortunately, Alignment contains the seeds of its own undoing. Well-aligned organizations ultimately fail because they lack the capacity to respond to the inevitable changes that occur in all operating environments. Thus, Alignment, by itself, leads to inflexibility and, eventually, organizational extinction. That is why the second—and equally important—task of leaders is to create the institutional capacity to engage in continuous renewal. This critical dimension of Adaptability requires leaders to use a different side of their brain than the side they employ when creating Alignment. Where Alignment is concerned with the disciplined, left-brain tasks of present performance (delivering high-quality products or services to existing customers and markets), Adaptability is focused on the creative, right-brain tasks of preparing for tomorrow (developing capabilities needed to survive in an uncertain future).

Thus, at a minimum, leaders must be mentally ambidextrous. While keeping the present system in alignment with one hand, leaders in highly adaptive organizations will, with their other hand, create the conditions under which followers will positively respond to events and trends in the external environment. Under these adaptive conditions, everyone in the organization will be appropriately innovative and embrace change.

Leadership is thus a bit like juggling two balls: Alignment and Adaptability. Of course, everyone knows that juggling only two balls is a simple feat—yet, at the same time, we know that leadership is an extremely difficult task. In fact, while successful leaders are juggling the two balls, they also are considering which of many additional balls they should pick up and put into play. They must carefully choose what new activities to pursue from a wide and bewildering menu of attractive options that followers put before them. They ask, "What new businesses should we be entering?" And, as if that weren't complicated enough, they must also be continually evaluating the viability (or longevity) of current activities. As Peter Drucker notes, successful leaders kill off one old activity for every new one they initiate. So leaders are not only constantly picking up new balls as they juggle, they are also continually putting down old ones. This requires considerable skill, dexterity, discipline, and foresight—as we can appreciate by analogy with the performance of circus jugglers. Truly talented jugglers stand behind a table and constantly pick up and put down various items of all sizes and shapes, and they often manage this feat while their assistants are throwing them new items that they must seamlessly integrate into the existing set of things they are juggling—all without dropping anything.

By extension, corporate leadership is a dynamic process of creating organizational Alignment around current activities while at the same time initiating new activities—and sloughing off, or abandoning, dying ones. When done well, leadership creates no discontinuities or crises (dropped balls). Indeed, the test of success is when observers witness a continuous flow of activity and fail to notice that, in fact, the set of balls in the air is constantly changing. In well-led organizations, Alignment and

Adaptability are seamless activities, and the institutional systems of rewards, planning, budgets, measurement, and the like serve simultaneously to reinforce both dimensions.

In contrast, poorly led organizations seldom get Alignment right and even more rarely do they manage the trick of Adaptability; and they never get the two elements to work in parallel. Instead, they are characterized by distinct periods in which all efforts are directed toward gaining Alignment, which leads to inflexibility, bureaucracy, and, ultimately, a crisis. Then, all efforts are turned toward the painful activity of revolutionary change in order to stave off the threat of extinction. The worst corporations lurch from crisis to inflexibility to crisis.

In sum, when both Alignment and Adaptability are equally present and mutually reinforcing, an organization is characterized by *strategic leadership*. [See Management of Change (vs. Strategic Leadership).]

Changing Oneself

Autobiographies and biographies of leaders almost all contain a description of a painful moment when the (usually young) protagonist learns from bitter experience that he or she has had entirely the wrong view about how one goes about creating followers. We read of the experience and wince because it would shatter the confidence of most of us, causing us to withdraw and vow never again to put ourselves on the line in pursuit of leadership. However, for the uncommon folk whose lives are the subjects of these volumes the event is, instead, *a glorious epiphany!* They learn from the experience, mend their ways, and go on to become leaders.

Countless examples of such career-defining moments have made it axiomatic that before leaders can change others, they must first change themselves. Unfortunately, the concept of "changing oneself" is almost always misinterpreted as "becoming someone else." Let's face facts: it might be possible for some individuals to alter their personalities after years of psychotherapy, but don't bet on it. Basic self-reinventions are extremely rare. It is hard enough to shake minor, embarrassing personal tics and flaws (I've been working unsuccessfully on a slight lisp for years); changing one's basic character is damn near impossible.

Leadership would be easier, of course, if we were more beautiful or handsome, a few inches taller, or if we had a deeper voice. Sorry. For such items you're stuck with the hand you were dealt. For most people it isn't even possible to change their "style"; witness Vice President Al Gore, who has devoted long hours in the fruitless pursuit of charisma.

Yet there are some things in our control. For starters, we can learn who we are and thus become comfortable with what we can't change. We can learn, moreover, how we are perceived by others and thus why we sometimes get puzzling responses that are the opposite of our intentions.

Most clearly and directly, we can change what we *do* as leaders. Here are a few of the easiest—and most important—things that everyone has the power to change. All would-be leaders can learn how to ask questions . . . and really listen to the answers; learn to involve people in decisions that affect them; learn to say "we" instead of "I"; learn to give credit to others; and learn to show real respect to everyone, including those who disagree with us.

Coherence

Japan's Sony and Holland's Philips are among the few corporations in the world that have all the essential components needed to succeed in the twenty-first century: they each are strong in computers, communications, software, and consumer electronics. Yet neither company has discovered how to get those pieces to work together. In both instances, the sum is less than the total of the parts. As Bruce Pasternack and Albert Viscio write in *The Centerless Corporation*, "successful companies in the future will be ones wise enough to harness the full potential of the entire organization."

And whose responsibility is it to make sure that all the pieces in an organization fit into a coherent whole, that knowledge is shared across boundaries, and that there is integration between strategy and rewards? And who must establish an overall structure and communicate a consistent message so that everyone in the company works toward the same goal? Pasternack and Viscio have the answer pegged: "The job of creating coherence is one of the major missions of the CEO. No one else can do it. It is a heroic leadership challenge."

While leaders don't do much, the alignment of strategy, structure, and processes is one leadership task that can*not* be delegated.

Resource: *Bruce A. Pasternack and Albert J. Viscio, *The Centerless Corporation* (New York: Simon & Schuster, 1998).

Commitment

Cynicism is the curse of our times. (See **A**pologia.) Healthy skepticism gave way long ago to contemptuous sneering at leaders who hold themselves to high moral standards. From Gandhi to Franklin Roosevelt, national leaders are now subject to debunking by historical revisionists who seek to discount all the accomplishments of those leaders who tried to do good. "If we only would take off our blinders and look close enough," the revisionists say, "we would find that even the Mahatma and FDR had serious character flaws." A thousand acts of public good are thus overbalanced by a single private misdeed. And the cynics are right by definition: if the standard of greatness is perfection, then, given the obvious imperfection of all mortals, there are no great leaders. Whew! Wouldn't it be *horrible* to have heroes?

Corporate leaders who attempt to behave in an ethical and socially responsible manner are likewise subject to scorn and derision. Such CEOs as Levi Strauss's Bob Haas, Herman Miller's Max DePree, and Malden Mills's Aaron Feuerstein are dismissed as naive do-gooders by *Wall Street Journal* editors who tell us that, unlike

Jack Welch and Al Dunlap, naive CEOs don't understand that "virtuous leadership" is an oxymoron! We all are much more comfortable, it seems, in the company of self-declared wolves than we are with flawed lambs who try to do good.

So it is with obvious reluctance that a corporate leader today dares in public to use such soft and suspect words as *morality, integrity, selflessness,* and *respect.* Even the seemingly tougher concept of commitment has an old-fashioned flavor to it— sounding like a value that Grandpa might have held dear but (heavens no!) *not* one that any virile, bottom-line-oriented, take-charge leader today would utter outside the context of a wedding vow.

To say that true leaders make commitments—to their principles, to their values, to their followers, and to themselves—seems not only anachronistic but preachy and soft-headed as well. We all know that, in the real world, commitments (like wedding vows) are made to be broken. William Bennett might make a career of expounding on the need for "virtue"—and the worst cynics, in particular, will buy his books, but they realistically give them to the only audience for whom they were intended: *children.* We thus limit concern with morality to the behavior of babes and to the confines of Sunday School. But *not* in the real world, no way!

Yet the fact remains that leadership requires commitment. Lincoln was a master of tactical wheeling and dealing—but he always did so in the context of his unremitting commitment to the principle of the preservation of the Union and to the principles of equality outlined by the nation's founders in the Declaration of Independence. H-P's David Packard, Motorola's Robert Galvin, IBM's Watsons (Sr. and Jr.) each, during many decades of leading their respective companies, never deviated an iota from their commitments to their values, principles, and philosophies of leadership. Ford's Donald Peterson, Corning's James Houghton, and Coca-Cola's Robert Goizueta committed themselves to long-term programs of strategic and cultural change in their organizations—and, years later, didn't waver on the promises they made to followers even when there was pressure from Wall Street and their boards to do so.

But we have to be judicious about whom we cite as an authority on matters of morals and values. So let's pick the toughest, most virile, least namby-pamby leader of the last score years or so: Margaret Thatcher. On the question of commitment, the Iron Lady was adamant: *One changes one's tactics, strategies, and programs as circumstances dictate; but change one's principles? Never.*

Communication

In a nutshell, here's how effective leaders spend their time: once they have set their organization's goals and strategies—and established appropriate plans, structures, and metrics to carry them out—leaders devote about half their time to developing people and half their time to communication.

But communicating *what?* The task of a leader is to communicate clearly and repeatedly the organization's vision, strategy, goals, and objectives, and to communicate its values, mission, purpose, and principles—all with the intent of helping every person involved understand what work needs to be done and why, and what part each individual plays in the overall effort.

That's fairly abstract, so let's look at what communication meant in practice in one successful company. W. L. Gore and Associates are the makers of Gore-Tex and other marvels of modern chemistry. The company's legendary founder, Bill Gore, was famous for practicing "nonmanagement": while he was alive, the company tolerated no hierarchy, no titles, no job descriptions, and no rules. There was reason behind Gore's apparent madness. The company had a single, overarching goal—

innovation—and, to achieve that end, Gore was committed to the elimination of all barriers, structures, and bureaucratic nonsense that would hamper the free play of employee imagination, creativity, and initiative.

Whenever a new Gore associate was hired, she was told to "go find something useful to do." Obviously, many people were a bit uneasy about such an open-ended assignment! They understandably craved more structure and clarity about what they were supposed to do. For example, new hires would often ask, "How much authority do I have?" To help them out, Gore would grab a piece of butcher paper and draw on it a stick figure boat floating on a wavy-line sea: "The boat is the company, and that's the waterline." He would then explain that every Gore associate had full authority to try anything, take any risk, make any decision, as long as it was "above the waterline." That way, if a mistake were made, the figurative hole could be patched up easily, and the ship could sail on without permanent damage. However, no one had authority to make a decision that affected the company "below the waterline" because that would risk sinking the entire ship. Gore would point out that the company might want to decide to take a bet-the-ship risk; however, since the consequences of such an action would affect everyone, that decision would have to be made collectively.

Got it? Although most Gore associates found the drawing helpful, in fact they still wouldn't fully grasp what Gore was telling them. They would ask, "That's all fine and good, but where's the waterline?" "Ah," Bill Gore would reply, "that's the question!" Because, of course, the waterline in any organization is always subjective, constantly moving, and dependent on varying circumstances. So Gore would then enter into a dialogue with his people, analyzing various hypothetical situations that they posed, engaging with them for as long as it took for a shared consensus to emerge about what a waterline decision, in fact, looked like. Such discussions took a very long time and were never concluded in one session, or in one day. In fact they were ongoing, and, in the process of conducting them, Gore was continually communicating and reinforcing the company's basic purpose, principles, and philosophy.

That's why communication takes at least 50 percent of a leader's time and effort. Indeed, Bill Gore spent close to *all* his time communicating, and there is no instance of a leader who ever spent too much time at this essential task. (See **S**ound Bites.)

Comparative Advantage
(Why Leadership Is Needed *Now* in Silicon Valley)

Question: Why don't leadership books ever describe the careers of the young Silicon Valley CEOs who have led their companies through multigazillion-dollar IPOs?

Answer: Because they aren't leaders.

If the response above sounds a bit flip, it's because there is no good short answer to that excellent question. To understand what is happening today in Silicon Valley, we first need to make clear distinctions between three separate kinds of comparative advantage: *technological, managerial,* and *leadership*.

Technological advantages tend to be quite dramatic. Thanks to several generations of brilliant entrepreneurs and inventors, Britain enjoyed the world's longest comparative technological advantage over its European competitors throughout the first half of the nineteenth century, which translated into enormous economic growth and political power for the nation. More briefly, the Soviet Union had a technological advantage in rocketry at the beginning of the Sputnik era. In the industrial arena, Ford

Motor held a technological advantage over all its competitors in the early part of the twentieth century (when it was the only auto manufacturer to have an assembly line). However, as these examples imply, it is difficult to maintain a purely technological advantage because competitors invariably catch up to the early leaders.

Managerial comparative advantages can be longer lasting. Germany and Japan overcame Britain's entrepreneurial and innovative brainpower with impressive managerial skill and discipline, which have given their industries a comparative advantage, on and off, for most of the last century. In the 1970s, managerial superiority allowed the United States to quickly overtake the Soviet Union's head start in space—and, more important, by building on those managerial skills it was able to create a steady stream of breakthroughs in aerospace technology. By the mid-1920s, GM's clear managerial superiority allowed it to surpass the more entrepreneurial Ford—and to maintain a leading position in the auto industry for decades to follow. Yet, in more recent years—as product cycles have shortened and the pace of change has quickened—comparative managerial advantages have become shorter in duration.

More and more, human organizations that thrive in the long term are ones that enjoy a *leadership* advantage. On the national level, during World War II the United States (with FDR and Eisenhower) and Britain (with Churchill and Montgomery) had clear leadership advantages over their Axis adversaries. More recently, Britain's remarkable national renaissance has coincided—not coincidentally, I believe—with the prime-ministership of Margaret Thatcher (and later that of Tony Blair).

Less controversial, perhaps, is the role of leadership in the corporate world. Throughout the 1980s and 1990s, various lists of "the world's most respected companies" remained remarkably constant, particularly given the volatility of world markets in the late 1990s: in Europe, it was Nestle, ABB, Daimler-Benz, and Ericsson; in Japan, it was Honda, Sony, and Toyota; and in the United States, it was GE, Intel,

Coca-Cola, and H-P. Significantly, each of those companies was known for its deep leadership capacity. Indeed, the comparative (and continually renewing) technological and managerial advantages those companies enjoyed resulted in great part from their profound leadership capabilities.

Now, we need to consider how the skills of five types of individuals— I. Engineers, II. Inventors, III. Entrepreneurs, IV. Managers, and V. Leaders—correspond with, and overlay, the categories described above. Although all five types are members of the same species (*Homo corporatus*), we need to recognize that they are seldom members of the same genus.

Silicon Valley, for example, is full of Types I through III—the brilliant (and frequently young) men and women who provide much of the current dynamism in the American economy and who lay the groundwork for the nation's future prosperity. In the early part of the twentieth century in the United States, Detroit was Silicon Valley, and the Midwest was similarly peopled by impressive young Types I, II, and III like Henry Ford (engineer, entrepreneur, inventor, and organizer par excellence) and GM's Billy Durant (investor, deal maker, and visionary without peer). There were many others as well, whose names we remember by the marques they left on the auto world: Olds, Studebaker, Champion, Buick, Chevrolet, Dodge, Fisher, Nash, Kaiser, and Willys. Famous names all; yet, significantly, not a leader in the bunch. In that regard, Silicon Valley is today about where the auto industry was circa 1920 (and where Britain was in the heyday of the Industrial Revolution).

Because proximity puts me at considerable risk, let me make the above as clear as possible: As a San Franciscan, I'm proud as punch that the Bay Area is currently the navel of the industrial universe. I like to brag that we have the nation's lowest unemployment and highest incomes as the result of Silicon Valley's cutting-edge technocorps. I particularly appreciate that the wealth created on the Peninsula has led to a renaissance in the Bay Area's educational and cultural institutions (not to mention the positive spillover on the quality of restaurants and cappuccino joints!). But what is needed *now* is to create a generation of Type Vs (leaders) to build on the glorious work of the brilliant Is, IIs, and IIIs. Silicon Valley needs to build a legacy that *lasts* (so that San Francisco doesn't end up in 2050 looking like Detroit in 2000).

Silicon Valley needs leaders who can work through other people in order to create institutions that are not dependent on them and who can create legacies of innovation and entrepreneurship that live on after they have retired (and even after they are dead and buried). Such leaders need to look forward to the future—and out beyond their company and industry to the broader communities of which they are a part. As brilliant an industrial organizer as Henry Ford was, his enterprise always revolved around him, depended on him, and, in the final analysis, was about *only* him. Leaders like Ford see themselves as bigger than their positions and, thus, create no worthy disciples. In this regard, Silicon Valley is more fortunate than Detroit in having had William Hewlett and David Packard as its pioneers and role models. In contrast to Ford, they created something bigger out of their positions as leaders of H-P: they created disciples; they created a culture of innovation that has survived for five decades; and they enlarged their industrial base to become civic leaders as well. Hewlett and Packard were engineers who learned to become managers, and, eventually, they grew to become leaders.

Henry Ford was an engineer and innovator who, like many current heads of Silicon Valley firms, never quite became a manager, let alone a leader (and although he left a fortune to bankroll what would become an admirable charitable institution, during his lifetime he exercised the opposite of civic engagement and moral leadership). The closest Detroit came to producing a Type V was Durant's successor at GM, Alfred P. Sloan. Yet, Sloan never fully grew out of the administrative (Type IV) role that he had created for himself, and, as a consequence, his legacy at General Motors was bureaucracy rather than a pipeline of leaders to build on the foundation he created. Although Silicon Valley may need a few more managers like Sloan, what it *really* needs now are leaders capable of harnessing and institutionalizing what Joseph Schumpeter called the entrepreneurial "cycle of creative destruction" and, thus, to avoid the bureaucratic fate of Sloan's Detroit.

So let's not confuse the manifest engineering and entrepreneurial talents of thirty-year-old technowhizzes who pocket megabucks in IPOs with the leadership skills of seventy-year-olds who have created institutions that will continue to innovate decades after their retirement. That doesn't mean that Type Vs are better than Types I, II, and III, nor does it mean that engineers can't grow into leaders. The point is that they are *different*—that it is a mistake to rush to acclaim young people for a skill they haven't had sufficient time to acquire.

What should today's thirty-something computer jockeys be doing to prepare themselves to grow from Type Is into Type Vs? One useful place to begin is with the three books that Andrew Grove has written over his long and successful career in Silicon Valley. Grove—the high-tech world's closest active approximation of Hewlett and Packard—wrote those three books at roughly fifteen-year intervals, and each instructively delineates an important phase in his personal and career development (and overlaps with the three stages of comparative advantage described above):

Phases I–II (Technological and Innovative). In 1963, Grove received his Ph.D. in engineering from UC Berkeley. He then began his professional career in the labs of Fairchild Instruments, where he participated in many of the major pioneering breakthroughs in semiconductors. He moved to Intel in 1967, where he continued to hone his technical skills. During this period, when his focus was solely on the lab and on technical questions, he wrote a widely used textbook on the physics of semiconductor devices.

Phases III–IV (Managerial and Entrepreneurial). During the 1970s, Intel grew rapidly as a firm, and Grove distinguished himself from many of his fellow scientists by successfully shifting his focus to meeting the entrepreneurial challenges of managing a growth company. He quickly progressed from being a researcher to managing a research team and, eventually, to managing the corporation's companywide research effort. In the process, his interests changed from technical questions to how to effectively manage time, people, and resources. Nonetheless, he applied his engineering discipline to his broader responsibilities, attempting to identify rules and logical methods for management. Grove drew on what he learned over the decade and organized those lessons in his best-selling 1983 book, *High Output Management*. The book was intended to help high-tech managers to organize their teams to become more productive and to leverage their own efforts to maximize their personal efficiency.

Phase V (Leadership). Grove became CEO of Intel in 1987, and, over the next decade, the company leapfrogged Motorola to become the world's largest producer of semiconductors. In 1996, his third book, *Only the Paranoid Survive,* marked yet another sea change in his career and professional emphasis. Whereas the word *leadership* never appeared in *High Output Management,* it had become the subject of the new work. And, unlike the previous books, *Paranoid* is almost entirely external in its focus and concerns. Here, Grove has little to say about what goes on inside a semiconductor or inside Intel's labs. Indeed, he is concerned only in passing with the internal management of the corporation. Now, his subject is the external environment; he writes about change, competitors, and customers. The theme of this book is *leadership*: how to create a great company and what to do to make certain that greatness will continue as the result of the ongoing culture of the organization. The scientific certainty found in his early books has now been replaced with the subjectivity of vision and risk taking, and the early concern with the here and now has been replaced with a focus on the long-term future.

It is important to recognize that in the 1960s the thirty-year-old Andy Grove could no more have written the third book than he could have been successful as CEO of Intel—as today he has lost his cutting-edge knowledge of science and could no longer write an authoritative text on physics. Young people with talent, technical expertise, and energy are capable of winning Nobel Prizes in physics; however, to create an institution that lasts requires the experience and breadth that come only through the long process of human growth.

Nonetheless, appropriately ambitious young people don't wait until they are fifty to start thinking like leaders. In fact, they start the process of development as early as possible. (See **T**omorrow's Leaders?) And as far as Silicon Valley is concerned, the more who successfully complete the career-long transition from engineer to leader, the better it will be for all in the long run. (See **F**ollowership.)

Resources: Andrew S. Grove, *High Output Management* (New York: Vintage Books, 1983).
*Andrew S. Grove, *Only the Paranoid Survive* (New York: Doubleday, 1996).

Contradictions, Anyone?

On the one hand, experts tell us that leadership is difficult—indeed, that it is the hardest of all social tasks to do well. On the other hand, the same experts claim that what leaders do is learnable—moreover, that it is "basic stuff." Isn't there a wee contradiction here? After all, if leadership is so simple and basic, why is it so difficult? To understand how both parts of that apparent contradiction can be true at the same time, we need to look both to science and to the arts as guides.

Science, in the form of social anthropology, helps us to understand how leadership is part of the human social contract. From the time the first bands of recognizably sapient humans organized themselves for purposes of safety, security, and the provision of food, there has been something approximating the role of leadership. Like other basic social elements—kinship, marriage, religion, sanctions and social control, and property relations—leadership has been an integral part of human culture everywhere. If, indeed, we are social animals, then it may be said that leadership is a part of our nature, a part of what it means to be human.

Then we must look to the arts for insight on what it means to be human. The earliest poetry, drama, and religious writings that have passed down to us through the millennia are remarkably consistent in that they all address the paradoxes, contradictions, and dilemmas of humans wrestling with the basics: being a good spouse or parent, telling the truth, doing a duty, and serving as a wise ruler. The timeless lesson of the arts is that getting this basic stuff right invariably trips us humans up— and as it has been that way, it always will be so. Few people consider their lives failures if they have not mastered the calculus, memorized Chinese ideograms, or learned how to play chess at a championship level. Instead, what we all struggle with—and gut-wrenchingly so—are our relationships with other people. In effect, then, the human condition is to struggle over the stuff that should be basic, natural, and easy.

So there is no more contradiction in saying that leadership is basic and difficult at one and the same time than in saying that marriage is basic and difficult. In his deeply philosophical—and moving—song "Anyone Can Whistle," Stephen Sondheim sums up this basic paradox of life: "What's hard comes easy / What's natural comes hard." (See **P**aradoxes.)

Controlling

Business textbooks used to define the tasks of management as planning, directing, motivating, and controlling. U.S. managers got the message—especially the controlling part—as Jan Carlzon, CEO of Scandinavian Airlines (SAS) learned firsthand in 1985. Carlzon had been invited by Warren Bennis to address two dozen of Los Angeles's most powerful executives on the campus of the University of Southern California.

Carlzon began his talk with an explanation of the sorry financial conditions he inherited at SAS, a description of the process of change he employed, and a review of the consequent results. He also described his philosophy of leadership, with specific reference to his now-famous notion of "turning the organizational pyramid upside down" so that leaders may serve followers. He explained why and how every SAS employee had been empowered—without the requirement of prior approval from supervisors—to do whatever was necessary to satisfy customers: "You can get people to develop their specific goals not by steering them with fixed rules but by giving them total responsibility to achieve a specific result." To get that result—namely, customer satisfaction—the key resource that employees needed was information: "An individual without information cannot take responsibility; an individual who is given information cannot help but take responsibility."

Carlzon then recounted examples of the exercise of such responsibility from the fifty million "moments of truth" that occurred annually when SAS employees had direct, one-on-one contact with customers. He argued that the sum total of those moments added up to the general level of satisfaction that had made the airline number one in Europe among business travelers.

At this point in the discussion, the executives started to grow fidgety. After much nervous coughing and paper shuffling, one CEO could take no more. Clearly enraged, he slammed his palm down on the table in front of him and, with the other hand, pointed an accusatory finger at the Swedish guest. "OK, Carlzon, now own up. How many of those fifty million moments went sour? How many times did your employees abuse the responsibility you gave them? How many times did somebody do something dumb that ended up costing your shareholders money?"

Carlzon took no offense at the interruption. Instead, he weighed his words carefully in reply: "Do you want the data from the first year or for the entire six years since we introduced the change?"

"The whole works. Come on, 'fess up!"

"I believe we have had about a half dozen serious instances of the type you mention. Those were times when employees went far beyond what was a reasonable effort on behalf of customers and, in so doing, caused costly errors."

Satisfied that he had made his point, the American turned to his peers and said, "There, I thought so. *That's* what you get when you let the lunatics run the asylum—anarchy!"

Politely, Carlzon mentioned that at SAS they thought that six errors in fifty million positive experiences was a pretty good ratio. Ignoring Carlzon's explanation, the interlocutor went back for more: "Now that you are shooting straight, tell us what you did about the employees who were ripping off your shareholders."

Either Carlzon didn't understand the CEO's vernacular or he couldn't believe his ears. "I'm sorry, what do you mean?"

"In plain English, how did you punish them?"

Carlzon got the drift. "Punish them? Why should we have punished them when it was *our* fault? We believe the task of leaders in a large company is to articulate the values of the organization, to create a system in which people can be productive, and to explain the goals that the system was established to achieve. We also believe that people don't act maliciously. If we in top management had done those jobs properly—if we had explained adequately the purpose behind employee empowerment—those few errors would not have occurred. That is why we went back to evaluate our own communication skills."

In essence, the U.S. manager saw his job as "controlling" the anarchic instincts of employees. In contrast, Jan Carlzon saw that the task of a leader as creating conditions under which followers will practice "self-control"—a far more powerful, effective, and ethical force.

Coda: As we now know, in the end Carlzon failed at SAS. (See **P**erfection.) His critics thus write off everything he accomplished beforehand, concluding that you can't learn anything positive from a flawed leader. Because all leaders are flawed, that's a dangerous assumption, and those who fail to learn from both how Carlzon successfully transformed SAS *and* how he ultimately self-destructed do so at their own peril.

Resource: *Jan Carlzon, *Moments of Truth* (New York: HarperCollins, 1987).

Controls

In the early 1920s, Du Pont's treasurer, John Jacob Raskob, moved his formidable managerial skills and creativity to General Motors. Among his many contributions to management was the invention of internal accounting systems. Thanks to Raskob's genius, managers ever since have been able to utilize standardized and quantified metrics to gauge how efficiently their company's resources are used and to objectively measure managerial performance. GM's comptrollers long used Raskob's system to prepare monthly ratings of the company's assembly operations. Although things may have changed recently, for nearly six decades some two dozen GM factories were ranked on an objective measure of productivity: the number of cars per hour that rolled off an assembly line. Managers whose factories regularly ranked near the top were rewarded with fat bonuses (and promotions), while those whose ratings consistently occupied lower rungs found future employment elsewhere.

Because the ratings were, in essence, competitive, an unintended consequence of GM's system was a strong disincentive for managers to share knowledge, to cooperate, or to help each other in any way. Those at the bottom were tempted to cut corners by stinting on quality in a panicked effort to push cars out the door. And those who didn't cheat complained bitterly that the "objective" system was, in fact, arbitrary and unfair because they had older factories, tougher unions, and so forth than did the "luckier" managers ranked at the top.

Today, ABB uses an internal accounting process, called ABACUS, that allows their comptroller in Zurich to collect data from the company's five thousand–odd profit centers around the world at the speed of sound and to analyze it at the speed of—if not light—certainly faster than Raskob ever dreamed possible. Yet, for all its speed and complexity, ABACUS is basically no more than an information-age update of Raskob's classic system. *The real difference is in the managerial behavior the two systems encourage.* At ABB, managers who are in competition with each other nonetheless cooperate, share best practices, and even rush to each other's aid when there is a problem. Moreover, ABB's managers not only say ABACUS is fair and objective, they sing its praises.

Why the difference? The comptroller at GM has historically been a financial number cruncher, while ABB's comptroller approaches the job from the perspective of people in operations. At GM, a central purpose of the internal accounting system is literally to *control* the behavior of managers by monitoring them closely and then to reward those who perform and punish those who don't. In contrast, the purpose of ABB's system is to identify problems and then to help managers solve them. At GM, there has been a winner-take-all rewards jackpot, while at ABB the differences in rewards between those ranked first, fiftieth, or five hundredth aren't so great that managers will beggar their peers—and screw up overall corporate performance—while trying to maximize their own bonuses. Although management by the numbers is a good idea when used appropriately (see **P**erformance), at GM "making your numbers" has been applied mindlessly as the sole measure of managerial efficiency. At ABB, in addition to making their numbers, managers are also evaluated on the basis of such criteria as cooperation, innovation, and flexibility. (See **G**enerosity.) And it is significant that the C in ABACUS stands for Communications and *not* Controls.

It is not difficult to fathom why things are different at ABB than at GM: ABB has been blessed with leadership, whereas GM has been run by a long line of managers since Raskob's boss, Alfred Sloan, retired in 1946. The absence of leadership at GM has left a vacuum that accountants, finance people, comptrollers, and other technicians have eagerly filled—in the process installing systems that have little rational link to the efficient making and selling of quality cars. In contrast, ABB's leaders have understood that their responsibility is to create a system in which the role of headquarters is to help people in decentralized units succeed in the absence of initiative-stultifying controls. They understand that leaders must drive change but that they will kill the initiative to change if they try to control it.

A ray of hope? ABB's Percy Barnevik has joined GM's board of directors. Will GM now listen, learn, and change? Tune in for the next exciting installment . . .

Conviction

Abraham Lincoln believed fervently in the preservation of the Union and in the principles found in the Declaration of Independence. Winston Churchill was passionate in his hatred of fascist tyranny. Margaret Thatcher was equally vehement about her abhorrence of communism. And, on a less lofty plane, Bill Gates believes down to his nerdy core everything he says about the future of technology and Microsoft's role in making it happen. Such zealous certainty about the rightness of one's cause is neither a luxury nor a nice-to-have leadership characteristic: *it is a necessity*.

Convictions are necessary because, without them, leaders would not be able to sustain the energy required to persevere. Leadership is so devilishly difficult—constant battering of pride and ego, two setbacks for every step forward, the burdensome responsibility for the welfare of others, the cross of unpopularity, the manifold risks—that only those who believe passionately in what they are doing can muster the will to get up morning after morning and resume the often thankless task. (See Resilience.)

Leaders also need convictions in order to attract and maintain followers. Sane people will not dedicate themselves to a cause, take a risk, put themselves on the line, or give extra effort if they sense a lack of conviction in their leaders. If leaders don't believe in what they are doing, why should followers? Moreover, followers have an uncanny ability to sense when those leaders who had formerly acted with certainty begin to harbor self-doubts. And conviction can't be faked because followers quickly ferret out phonies.

Conviction, then, helps provide the energy, focus, consistency, persistence, optimism, obsession, patience, and resilience needed to lead. In matters of leadership, convictions count for even more than brains. In describing the creative pressure cooker in which Disney executives do competitive battle—pitching ideas and arm wrestling over whose project gets funded—Michael Eisner is alleged to have said, "A strong point of view is worth twenty I.Q. points."

Can you learn to *do* conviction? Obviously not. But leaders can learn to say only that which they believe.

Coolidge Syndrome

There are three sure symptoms of leadership deficiency in an organization.

Symptom #1: Not Working. This is a reliable indicator of the dreaded Coolidge Syndrome.

Reporter:	Mr. President, how many people work for you at the White House?
Calvin Coolidge:	Oh, about half of them.

In the 1920s, it might have been an acceptable level of performance when only 50 percent of Silent Cal's crew had their oars in the water. However, in today's corporate world, the minimum requirement is for all employees not to be merely engaged but to be pulling in unison. What the thirtieth president of the United States didn't get was that *he* was the source of the low output in the White House. Why should his staff have been hard at work if he wasn't?

Symptom #2: Doing the Wrong Thing. At the Ford Motor Company in the early 1980s, everybody was hard at work . . . doing their own thing. People worked hard, all right; problem was, they weren't doing the right things, and they weren't doing things that were useful to the overall good of the company. Ford was a concatenation of hard-working silos, smokestacks, fiefdoms—call them what you will—each going its own way. Those individual chunks of turf produced about $3 billion worth of red ink between 1980 and 1982.

Who was at fault: the line? the staff? the union? Ford tried all sorts of fixes, ranging from fiats by Henry Ford II (a.k.a. "Henry the Lesser") through incentives and restructurings to threats of bodily mutilation. Nothing worked until, one day in the mid-1980s, the two leaders who were vying for the CEO post changed *their* behavior. When all else failed, Donald Peterson and Red Poling got together and decided to cooperate instead of compete with each other. And, lo and behold, others down the line followed suit! (See **J**oint Leadership.)

Symptom #3: Working to Rule. The only thing worse for an organization than having people who don't do what they are told is having employees who do exactly what they are told (and nothing more). Sweden's Jan Carlzon, former CEO of SAS, learned that lesson the hard way, as he confessed in *Moments of Truth,* his candid account of how he became a leader.

At the age of thirty-two, Carlzon found himself president of an SAS subsidiary with fourteen hundred employees. Inexperienced and unsure of himself, he decided to "take charge" like the leaders he had read about in business magazines: "So I began acting the way I thought a boss should act." He barked detailed orders, told people how to do their jobs, and "no matter what the situation, I'd deliver my edicts: 'Now I want this!'. . . I made countless decisions with very little knowledge, experience, or information." The employees loyally and obediently did exactly what he told them to do, and performance and profits drooped accordingly.

As things went from bad to worse, he raised hell about the lack of motivation and initiative until, one day, a frank and courageous employee "who had suddenly been 'demoted' by my management style" explained the facts of leadership to his boss. Carlzon then discovered that "the company was not asking me to make all the decisions on my own, only to create the right atmosphere, the right conditions for others to do their jobs better. I began to understand the difference between a traditional corporate executive, who issues instruction after instruction from the top, and the new corporate leaders, who must set the tone and keep the big picture in mind."

At a young age Carlzon learned from experience that effective leaders set aside that culturally conditioned "natural" instinct to lead by push, particularly when times are tough. True leaders instead adopt the unnatural behavior of always leading by the pull of inspiring values.

Resources: *R. T. Pascale, *Managing on the Edge* (New York: Simon & Schuster, 1990).
*Jan Carlzon, *Moments of Truth* (New York: HarperCollins, 1987).

D

LEADERSHIP
A to Z

Definition of Leadership

There are dozens of definitions of leadership—some banal, some controversial, but most of them flawed by being either incomplete or too complex. Not surprisingly, our beliefs about who leaders are and what they do is reflected in the definitions we use. Our pet theory (see Theories of Leadership) will thus drive the definition we offer, often unconsciously.

Peter Drucker cuts through this subjectivity with a fine example of Occam's Razor. In searching for the simplest definition, he asks the basic question, What is it that all leaders have in common? On first blush, Drucker's answer to his own question may seem simplistic—even tautological. He tells us that all leaders have only one thing in common: *followers*. On second thought, we start to appreciate that there is something profound in his insight.

Building on this minimalist definition of a leader as "someone with followers," Drucker is then able to identify the prime role of leadership. In a nutshell, he tells us that the role of a leader is to create followers. Understanding this, would-be leaders can focus their efforts on learning what they must *do* in order to attract followers. There is no more practical starting point.

Delegation

When Ken Macke was CEO of the Dayton Hudson Corporation back in the 1980s, he was walking through the company's flagship Dayton's department store in Minneapolis when he noticed that the once-popular tearoom had two elderly customers being served by three somnolent waiters. On the way out, he also took note of the fact that the store's new yogurt counter—staffed by one harried yogurt jerk—was mobbed by some thirty young customers. Most managers would have responded by grabbing two of the employees in the tearoom and shoving them behind the yogurt bar, where they could be more productive. But Macke did nothing. He didn't even call the president of Dayton's to tell him what he saw. He explained, "If I had jerked the president's wire, he would have jerked the store manager's wire, and he would have jerked the floor manager's wire; . . . pretty soon, everybody down to the yogurt jerk would be standing around depending on me to play puppeteer."

Macke recognized that, with more than a hundred thousand employees in hundreds of stores in all fifty states, there was no way he could "manage" every employee's behavior. All he could hope to do was to create the conditions in which they would assume the responsibility to do right by customers. Macke thus practiced "leadership by example," believing that if he demonstrated trust in the people who reported to him, they in turn would trust their direct reports . . . and so on down the line.

Macke also practiced "leadership by walking around," but he did it in a fashion quite unlike the big-ego executives who run around doing everyone's job *for them*. Instead, Macke removed obstacles that prevented his people from doing *their own* jobs, and he enabled them to take individual bottom-line responsibility. He spent his time nurturing worthy successors and creating structures, systems, and habits of mind that lived on at all levels of the organization long after he retired.

Macke believed that Dayton Hudson became the nation's fastest growing retailer through commitment to high standards of customer service and ethical principles. That's why he devoted himself to communicating those standards—while leaving the details to the folks in the trenches, even if they made an occasional mistake (see **D**etails). He understood that, ultimately, the company depended on the lowest level employees to serve its customers.

The late E. F. Schumacher described the principle of delegation in this way: "The structure of the organization can be symbolized by a man holding a large number of balloons. . . . The man does not lord it over the balloons, but stands beneath them holding all the strings firmly in his hand. Every balloon is not only an administrative unit, but also an entrepreneurial unit." That was Ken Macke's leadership philosophy.

Resources: James O'Toole, *Vanguard Management* (New York: Doubleday, 1985).
E. F. Schumacher, *Small Is Beautiful* (New York: HarperCollins, 1973).

Denial
("What Hump?")

The chairman of the board of a large financial institution rang up the other day. He called to vent frustration about his repeated attempts to convince the company's CEO that he had serious leadership problems. It seems the exec veeps were all up in arms, calling board members to complain that the CEO was a closed-minded, inflexible tyrant whose behavior would soon cause newly recruited talent to walk. The chairman explained, "When I've tried to warn our CEO about this, he confidently reassures me, 'Don't worry, I've got a loyal team squarely behind me.' And you, know, *he really believes things are OK.*"

In the Mel Brooks film *Young Frankenstein,* Dr. Frankenstein offers a few words of sympathy to Igor, his terribly misshapen, hunchbacked assistant. Igor replies, "Hump? What hump?"

Being honest with ourselves is one of life's most difficult challenges. Doubtless, we all kid ourselves into believing that we are better golfers, singers, and lovers than we are. Although a little denial on that order is harmless (and may even give one's ego a necessary boost), leaders who deny reality about their businesses—and, especially, about themselves—imperil both their organizations and their own careers. And leaders who establish systems in their businesses *the function of which is to deny reality* are committing inexcusable folly. Yet it's the exceptional organization that is free of comforting misperceptions about itself and its environment, and the exceptional leader who is truly honest with himself.

One entrepreneur I know has a small, relatively successful business employing some twenty-five people. A prime duty of them all, apparently, is to reassure the boss how smart he is. His first product was a resounding success, but the second product has been a bust. His employees have reacted to this failure by telling the boss that his customers are ignorant and his competitors have formed a conspiracy against him. In fact, the failed product is an ever-so-slight variation on the first, smash-hit product—the sort of product everyone wants one of, but no sane person could possible use two. Last I heard, the boss's troops were encouraging his manic efforts to try yet another variation on the initial product.

Surrounding oneself with sycophants, killing bearers of bad news, rewarding those who reaffirm our prejudices, and building belief systems that reinforce what we want to hear are all common failings of leaders in organizations small and large. General Motors, for example, has institutionalized a set of managerial beliefs about its customers, workers, foreign competitors, and the government that causes the company to self-inflict nasty wounds with predictable regularity. Whatever problem GM faces, it is always blamed on "them." Hence, it doesn't occur to GM's leaders to address the true, underlying cause of their perpetual woes: a culture that rejects leaders who advocate fundamental change.

It happens everywhere. All companies are prone to embrace outmoded premises that, in time, will do them in. Remember how Kodak and Polaroid charged ahead with chemical- and mechanical-based products in the face of overwhelming evidence that their competitors were ready to market advanced electronic alternatives? Why didn't somebody at those companies utter the obvious? And on it goes. . . .

What can be done about this persistent pattern of denial? In the 1980s, Verne Moreland, then an executive at NCR, half-facetiously proposed that companies appoint one individual to function in the role the "fool" used to play in royal courts. The official corporate fool would be given license to "disturb with glimpses of confounding truth, . . . to challenge by jest and conundrum all that is sacred and all the savants have proved to be true and immutable." In fact, Moreland anticipated the growing trend among CEOs to hire "coaches"—individuals who are not part of the regular organization and, thus, are free to tell the boss what he or she may not want to hear from subordinates.

When Corning's James Houghton began his career as CEO, he had the good sense to hire Forrest Behm, an about-to-retire executive, to coach him in his efforts to lead the transformation of the company. Houghton was a quick study, and as soon as he had internalized what he had to do to become an effective leader, Behm retired—and Jamie went on to rack up a brilliant record as a master of change. (See Transforming Leadership.)

Of course, the ideal solution is to license *everybody* to play the fool. Great leaders create a climate of openness in which it is the norm to challenge assumptions (and, hence, it is neither disrespectful nor threatening to the boss to tell the truth). At Radica, the makers of innovative electronic games, CEO Bob Davids has turned orthodox corporate behavior on its ear by offering the greatest rewards to employees who put the lie to sacred cows and demonstrate that the emperor wears no clothes—even if the emperor turns out to be the CEO himself. "We pay extra for people who push back," David explains.

This openness to threatening ideas allowed Radica to quickly abandon a product strategy that Davids had developed and to move into a new line of business that permitted the company to more than triple its sales in the space of a year. Leaders who go this route run the risk of occasional embarrassment; nonetheless, they should be willing to pay the occasional cost of diminished ego. After all, it's far better than losing their pants to their competitors!

Details

"God is in the details." That's what the architect Ludwig Mies van der Rohe is reported to have said. Experts on leadership often quote Mies with the intent of reminding would-be leaders that greatness comes from paying attention to the smallest details—even those things that the casual observer would overlook. That message is often reinforced by a related story about another great architect, Antonio Gaudi, who designed the famous cathedral in Barcelona. Legend has is that, early in construction of the cathedral, Barcelona's cardinal called on Gaudi to complain that cost overruns were getting out of hand: "Antonio, why do you have to put expensive statues of angels on the roof where nobody will ever see them!" Gaudi replied, "God will notice."

Granted, it sounds logical to extend that inspiring lesson about greatness in the visual arts to the art of leadership. But in this case the analogy doesn't quite work. If one observes the causes of failure among leaders, it would be more accurate to say *the devil is in the details.*

Take GM's storied former CEO, Roger Smith, as a case in point. Smith was a master of details. He could match the sharpest accounting minds in manipulating financial ratios and in fly-specking balance sheets with decimal points to six places. He knew where the profits were, who was meeting their targets, and what the return was on every model of Delco battery.

What Smith didn't have was a clear understanding of the big picture: he lacked a "concept of the corporation" in the words of GM's founder, Alfred Sloan. Call it vision, purpose, or mission, Smith didn't know what he was trying to achieve in the end. So he concentrated his efforts on the here and now—and on a lot of details that, in hindsight, were a waste of time, misdirected, and, in many cases, counterproductive. One of my students once wrote an essay in which he concluded that Hamlet kept putting off avenging the murder of his father because he was "too busy doing other stuff." Smith was Detroit's Hamlet.

So here's a better analogy of leadership to art: great artists know exactly what to do with the details because they can clearly visualize the end state—they see the finished picture in their minds. Unlike the extremely busy Mr. Smith, leaders don't actually need to *do* very much. They don't need to make a lot of decisions, don't need to tell people how to do their work, and don't need to make, sell, or design anything themselves. In fact, to the extent they don't do such operational things, they have more time to concentrate on the real work of leadership. And one of the absolutely indispensable things that leaders must do is to keep an eye on the big picture.

Every day, leaders must define and communicate the basic purpose of the organization. To do so, leaders must be able to answer the following questions: *What business are we in? How do we measure success? What is our mission? To what end do we do what we do?* By thus keeping an eye on the ball, leaders focus the actions of everyone else in the company. After all, most important strategic questions come down to, *Should we do this or should we do that?* The only way one can answer such questions is in the context of the ultimate target or goal. Leaders thus help the organization sort out the important from the unimportant, the relevant from the peripheral, and thereby keep the ship on course. But they can't do that if they are lost in the details.

In sum, by focusing on the big picture, leaders know what the details should look like when they see them. And when leaders focus on the big picture, everyone *else* knows what to do about the details. In fact, by focusing on the big picture, leaders don't have to worry about the details at all because everyone else is!

Differences

All leadership situations are different. Obviously, organizations differ in terms of industry, products, culture, tradition, age, and the strategic challenges they face. Leaders themselves have different personalities, styles, and abilities. And leaders all start from different places and use different techniques and processes to bring about change. For example, in their respective companies, British Petroleum's John Browne began by breaking down the hierarchy, GE's Jack Welch began by offering a strategy ("Be #1 or #2"), Kodak's George Fisher set out to strengthen the balance sheet, and H-P's Lew Platt stressed the need for more product innovation. Such differences are critical, and good leaders recognize them and act accordingly.

In contrast, poor leaders are insensitive to the contingencies of the challenges they face and, thus, misdirect their energies. Because the differences inherent in the situations organizations face appear so obvious and overpowering, the vast majority of leaders get caught up in dealing with those contingent complexities. In so doing, they can't see the forest for the trees: they lose sight of what they must *do* themselves as leaders in order to be successful. Sadly, the academic approach to leadership focuses on differences, magnifying their importance and adding to the confusion managers clearly experience as the result of the complexities they face. The prevailing academic theory of contingency leads to the creation of a litany of factors that differs from situation to situation, about which little that is useful can be said in general.

Similarly, the academic fixation on "style" leads to the obvious conclusion that every leader is different and that little can be done about one's basic personality. Because leaders can't change the organizational challenges they face and can't change who they are, academic counsel thus causes them to throw up their hands in despair and to do nothing. Worse, it causes poor leaders to reject the experience of others because "my situation is *different.*" Thus, they never learn.

Truly effective leaders understand that, despite all obvious differences, not everything is situational. Oracle's President and COO, Ray Lane, teaches his high-tech troops to think about "consistent values; different styles." He thus helpfully differentiates the effective use of different styles to communicate with diverse audiences, on the one hand, from amoral, situational leaders, on the other.

Effective leaders understand that there are some things that every leader must *do* in order to create followers and to create aligned and adaptive organizations. Although they can't change the challenges they face—or change their personalities—they recognize that they can learn to do things that will make them more effective in playing the hands they were dealt. And they understand that the first place to look when seeking to learn how to do those things is to the successful experience of others. Recognizing that those experiences will never be exactly the same as their own, they ask, "What general pattern can I draw from experience, and what can I do given my situation?"

Dunlap, "Chainsaw" Al
(the Real Lesson)

When Sunbeam's board gave Al "Chainsaw" Dunlap his long-overdue comeuppance in the summer of 1998, the event was subject to as much instant analysis in the press as the death of Princess Diana had received a year earlier. In both instances, the amount of punditry failed to compensate for its manifest lack of depth.

The common wisdom about Dunlap's leadership was neatly summed up by two well-credentialed commentators in *The New York Times*. They concluded that Ol' Al is just "a one-trick pony" who knows how to do turnarounds but lacks the skills to "create and sustain consistently high growth." In effect, these experts did a riff on the standard contingency-theory theme. They concluded that the leadership lesson to be learned from the Sunbeam fiasco was that leaders the likes of Al are fine when you want to cut costs, but such Johnny-One-Notes are "unable to size up each new situation and act accordingly." Ergo, when choosing leaders, they advised corporate boards to "look for versatility."

Versatility is doubtless a useful leadership trait, but is that really what we learn from all of Chainsaw's buzzin', slashin', and ultimate self-destruction? The common wisdom falls short of useful insight because it rests on a fundamental misunderstanding of the role, responsibility, and function of leadership. If all the many definitions of leadership have anything in common it is simply that *leaders act through other people.* By definition, leadership is never a solo act. Thus, it is the common task of all leaders to create followers. (See **D**efinition of Leadership.)

By Al Dunlap's own account of his experience in the many companies he has headed, he emphatically rejects working through others. Instead, trusting no one, he proudly calls all the shots himself. His two favorite words are *I* and *me.* He writes that his modus operandi on taking over an ailing company is (a) to review the balance sheet, (b) to identify the poor performing parts of the business, then (c) to take personal charge of ordering factory closings, head-choppings, and sell-offs of the dogs that damage the bottom line. Certainly other managers appear as characters in Dunlap's tale (he gleefully describes firing top executives based on his fleeting first impressions of them), but nowhere does he talk about creating followers, enlisting them in his vision, or even soliciting information (much less advice) from them.

What Al does is make tough decisions. And, without doubt, there are times when leaders have to make tough, even courageous, decisions. Sometimes leaders have to sell off businesses, close factories, and lay off high-performing executives who behave in ways that are inconsistent with the values of the organization. (See **H**angings, Public.) Indeed, if they shy away from such decisions, they will be ineffective and, thus, poor leaders. But making a tough decision is not, in itself, an act of leadership (if it were, judges would be thought of as leaders).

However, the manner in which one makes a tough decision may make it an act of leadership. For example, when Chief Justice Earl Warren decided to rule against school desegregation in the 1950s, he assumed a leadership role not only within the court but in the broader society as well. His leadership consisted of building the case for change, overcoming resistance, and getting buy-in from opponents by showing them how the nation, as a whole, would be better off if all its citizens had equal opportunity. For that he is remembered as a leader and not just as a judge.

In contrast, Dunlap never bothers to create a constituency, never bothers to create a vision that others can take as their own, and never bothers to try to change behavior. Hence, the real lesson is, *Al Dunlap isn't a leader.*

Resources: David A. Nadler and Donald C. Hambrick, "Viewpoint," New York Times, July 5, 1998, p. 10 (Business Section).

Albert C. Dunlap with Bob Andelman, *Mean Business* (New York: Times Books, 1996).

LEADERSHIP
A to Z

Early Wins

Followers are a fickle lot. They easily fall in and out of love with their leaders, often changing allegiance with no more justification than the appearance on the scene of an attractive new suitor. Nonetheless, followers make legitimate demands on their leaders (for example, by refusing to follow those who are ineffective). If leaders can't make good on promises, if they can't deliver the goods, if they fail to take an organization to a better place, followers will lose faith and be followers no more.

That's because legions of followers know through bitter experience that leaders always woo us with seductive visions—corporate CEOs promise training to employees, growth to investors, and service to customers, while politicians promise everybody lower taxes and, as a fillip, the moon—but few make good on their pledges. As a consequence, we are skeptical, if not downright cynical, whenever we hear would-be leaders swear oaths, give their word, offer assurances, or take vows. We say, "Promises, promises . . . what we want is action!"

It is through their accomplishments that leaders gain credibility. And each time they deliver, they build allegiance and accrue commitment among followers.

The effect is cumulative: more accomplishments mean more and longer-lasting loyalty. Given followership's brief half-life, leaders who are new on the job look to demonstrate their effectiveness as early as possible during that honeymoon period in which most followers are willing to give leaders a fair chance to prove themselves. Hence, before loyalty begins to erode, leaders seek to cement relationships with followers by making good on a promise or by demonstrating in one way or another that they have the ability to make things happen.

In fact, leaders often find it far easier to accomplish change—particularly to do hard things—earlier, rather than later, in their tenures. The common wisdom has it that the ability to bring about change is almost a direct function of time in office.

Yet, although every effective leader is sensitive to the importance of early wins, the great ones don't give up if they don't immediately realize their agendas, and they don't throw up their hands if conditions change late in their careers. Indeed, timid leaders use timing as a convenient excuse for not acting—or for putting off the burden of change until the next person's watch. They turn the truism *It is imperative to act during the first hundred days in office* into a hard and fast law and thus do nothing after the first three months—then they congratulate themselves for obeying the law!

Just because something is hard doesn't mean it is impossible or that it doesn't need to be done. What is impressive about the likes of Intel's Andy Grove, Apple's Steve Jobs, and PeopleSoft's Dave Duffield is that they have been as willing to lead major changes late in their careers as they were at the beginning, when, admittedly, there was less inertial resistance. Real leaders acknowledge the contingencies of timing, but they don't look for excuses.

Effectiveness

Effectiveness is the sine qua non of leadership, the minimum that followers have a right to expect from leaders. Followers measure the effectiveness of leaders by their ability to deliver the goods: Newt Gingrich commits to a balanced budget, Jack Welch commits to a certain financial return to investors, Gandhi commits to Indian independence, Churchill commits to victory over Germany, Lyndon Johnson commits to waging a war on poverty, Al Dunlap commits to turning around a failing business, Richard Nixon commits to ending the Vietnam war, Bill Gates commits to creating new technological marvels, and General George Patton commits to whipping the panzer division in Sicily. Different causes these, yet we take the measure of all leaders by the same single standard: the extent to which they bring about whatever they set out to accomplish. *Effective leaders achieve their goals,* we say. For most leaders, that's all followers ask of them.

Doubtless, the measure of effectiveness is, and must be, the least common denominator of leadership. For how could we call someone a leader who is manifestly ineffective? To be an effective leader is, by definition, to be competent. Yet, is effectiveness the sum of it all? More to the point, *should it be* the end all, the totality, of leadership?

If Nixon ends the war in Vietnam, if Patton liberates Europe, if Gingrich balances the budget, if Dunlap turns around Sunbeam, are we then satisfied with their leadership? Perhaps . . . yet, perhaps not. For some followers, at least, effectiveness is not enough; they will also want to evaluate their leaders on a moral dimension. It is easy to see the moral issue in extreme cases: Mao, Stalin, and Mussolini were all effective in achieving their goals. But because their behavior and the ends they sought were damaging to their own people, few observers would cite them as exemplary leaders.

Less extreme examples are more problematic: Patton was Dwight Eisenhower's most effective general; nonetheless, Ike decided to reprimand Patton and to withhold appointing him to a high command because of his serious and frequent lapses of moral judgment. In the end, Eisenhower decided that leadership—at least in his army—had a moral as well as an effectiveness dimension.

More difficult yet is the case of Al Dunlap, who, to some investors on Wall Street, is a great leader because he delivers on his financial commitments. And the same can be said of the most difficult case of all, Jack Welch. His many admirers evaluate his leadership by the single measure of the return he provides GE's investors. It is irrelevant, they say, that he abused managers early in his career, causing grown men to cry (and one poor soul even to soil his trousers as the result of a public berating by Welch).

Who is right, those who, like Eisenhower, see leadership as a multidimensional activity with a strong moral component or those who, like Welch, see leadership as unidimensional and, thus, reducible to being measured solely in terms of effectiveness? Choosing which definition is correct—and then conducting one's self in accordance with that conviction—is the most difficult single moral choice that all leaders must make for themselves. Each leader must ask, "How do I want others to judge me? How do I want to judge myself?" Nobody ever said leadership is easy.

Ego

L eadership has its dark side. The malignant actions of this century's numerous tyrants have created an understandable ambivalence about leadership in the minds of many thoughtful observers. And some aspects of what passes as "acceptable" leadership behavior are, in truth, far from benign.

In the United States, in particular, there is undeserved tolerance today for harmful displays of arrogance and ego among leaders in all professions. The actions of former Washington, D.C., mayor Marion Barry are only the extreme manifestation of this behavior. In the Congress, in business, in the press, and in sports, leaders today frequently step over the line of self-confidence to engage in shows of narcissism that would have been considered bad manners, at the least, in eras less given to self-absorption.

For example, the coach of the U.S. soccer team forgot that his is a team sport, and the result was a disastrous showing for the United States in the 1998 World Cup. One team member (who requested anonymity) explained to reporters how the coach's egotism destroyed the team's chemistry: "The reason we're upset is we got this guy his job. He talks about trust and sacrifice, and most of the time, we're still talking about 'we' and he's talking about 'I,' he's taking credit for all the things we accomplished as a group in soccer. Everything we worked for, everything we accomplished, is thrown away not because of talent but because he wanted it to be his show."

Even such fine business leaders as Jack Welch and Michael Eisner frequently skirt disaster by arrogantly behaving as if their company's successes were "their show" alone. Eisner, who can be genuinely humble in private, is given to embarrassing public displays of narcissism when he represents Disney at press conferences and other open forums. And his arrogance has consequences: his self-defeating hiring (and subsequent expensive firing) of Michael Ovitz is but one item in a long list of examples of his hubris overcoming his reason (in a CEO who was less successful financially the flaw would be fatal).

And it should have been a tip-off to the U.S. electorate that they were dealing with an out-of-control ego when Bill Clinton admitted, during the 1994 campaign, that he had single-mindedly pursued the U.S. presidency from the day he met John F. Kennedy thirty years earlier. Clinton wanted to be president, we later learned, not because there was an agenda that needed to be accomplished; no, he hungered for the ego satisfactions of the presidency. He wanted to be *the* leader, and it was as simple as that. His ambition was clearly inappropriate.

As Plato understood twenty-five hundred years ago, we should be wary of those who want desperately to lead for the sake of leading. When leadership ambition, like Gandhi's, is directed toward achieving an end, it is both noble and necessary. But ambitious leadership that is about nothing more than the glorification of the self is both unseemly and potentially dangerous.

Because we live in an era in which self-promotion, self-glorification, and self-indulgence are the norm, we tend not to notice the telltale signs of an inflated ego until it is too late. We should be more sensitive to the threat. Unfortunately, much of the current fascination with the topic of leadership—the hundreds of new college courses and, alas, even books such as this one—can easily degenerate into fodder for the advancement of that ungodly trinity of me, myself, and I. Surely, the United States needs more and better leadership. And it is good for society, organizations, and individuals themselves when they step up and accept the responsibility to be *a* leader. But it is unhealthy in the extreme for all concerned when the individual's goal is simply to be *the* leader of something—or of anything.

That's why you should start with a little self-assessment: "Do I want to be a leader to achieve a special goal, or am I just after the satisfaction of being in a leadership position? Do I want to be a leader, or am I really only interested in being *the* leader?" Remember, *appropriate* ambition is directed toward achieving the goals of an institution and realizing the needs of followers.

Energy

What is the value-added of leadership? Many effective leaders don't create the strategies for their organizations, most don't do the actual work of change, and few are involved in day-to-day operational decision making, *so what's their contribution?* Based on casual observations of leaders at work, one might conclude that, in most organizations, they are superfluous, marginal contributors or, at worst, expendable overhead!

And if one's frame of reference were a symphony orchestra, the judgment even might be harsher because conductors appear to be little more than expensive frills. Anyone who has ever observed the members of an orchestra during a performance has been struck by the fact that the musicians seldom look at the conductor. Hell, most musicians appear blissfully unaware that a wild-haired person is standing before them on a podium, gesticulating madly, pointing a menacing baton at them, and, in general, carrying on with histrionic behavior that, in any other venue, would get that person committed to the funny farm.

The violinists couldn't care less: they concentrate intently on reading their music and on taking their lead from the first violin. The oboists seem to be saying, "Just ignore him." Even the underemployed timpanist—whose one brief moment in the spotlight requires entering the fray at exactly the right split second—will be observed looking down at his kettle drums when the conductor dramatically offers him his cue. Indeed, except for giving the downbeat at the start of a piece—a job the concertmaster could do just as easily—the function of the conductor seems limited to amusing the audience, who, otherwise, would have little to look at during the concert.

While moderating a seminar at the renowned Aspen Music Festival, I decided to put the question squarely to a group of talented musicians: "What use is a conductor, anyway?" They debated the question for half an hour before arriving at a consensus. To a person, the musicians agreed that no necessary function is performed by a conductor's baton pointing and arm waving; nonetheless, they were convinced that conductors make all the difference in the world to the overall quality of a performance.

The musicians cited experiences they had had with various conductors: "Listen to a recording of Mahler. You can tell in an instant if it was conducted by Leonard Bernstein; it's that much better." "When James De Priest [Seattle Symphony's conductor] leads the Aspen student orchestra, we sound like seasoned professionals." "[San Francisco Symphony's] Michael Tilson Thomas brings out the best in the orchestra, taking us to heights we hadn't dreamed possible." In sum, the musicians came to the general conclusion that *the conductor energizes an orchestra.*

Like symphony orchestras, all groups and organizations are capable of getting by without leadership. Players in a pickup game of basketball don't need a coach; universities function quite smoothly even when there is as much as a two-year vacancy in the president's office; and government agencies get along for decades when headed by administrative placeholders. *But all high-performing organizations have leadership.*

The Disney corporation, for example, limped along leaderless for years after Walt Disney died, making a little money on its library of films and even carrying out a few new projects like Epcot. But when Michael Eisner brought his enormous store of energy to Disney's Burbank headquarters, the tone and pace of the place changed so dramatically that people who formerly were satisfied with being good now would settle for no less than being great. (See **Q**uestions.)

Leaders energize organizations by allowing their own natural enthusiasm to emerge and by sharing their strong convictions about what might be, should be, and could be (if everyone's effort and commitment were engaged). There is an undeniable element of cheerleading in this. After all, the natural emotional state of any group tends to regress toward flatness over time. Groups aren't naturally enthusiastic about doing *anything*. (Remember how hard it was to get the old gang to get off their duffs and go to the beach, a ballgame, or a movie? All they wanted to do was "hang out" listlessly wherever they were.) The job of the leader is to get a group moving, to get them to do something they are going to be happier doing, and to get them involved in the fun of doing something more worthwhile.

In light of this, it is odd to find so many leaders who try to suppress their own enthusiasm in order to appear cool, unengaged, and "above" optimism and eagerness. This doesn't mean leaders are phonies who fake enthusiasm or, like Tom Sawyer, hype the "fun" of whitewashing a fence. Leaders can show enthusiasm in many different ways, but what is important is that it be authentic and not hidden (and when there is no wellspring of natural enthusiasm to tap, that's probably a sign that they are doing the wrong thing).

When Alan Mulally was leading the team of seven thousand people who designed and built the Boeing 777, he was personally excited about the prospect of creating the best airplane in the world. He defined his leadership task as communicating that enthusiasm: "We want everyone to feel that, *oh, boy*, building a brand-new airplane would be worth contributing to! The mission has to be bigger than any one of us, and it has to feel good. Making a new generation of airplane feels like a really good thing. It's meaningful. So that became our mission: building the best new airplane we possibly could."

Some may feel that's gooey talk coming from an engineer who has his master's degree from MIT and is a Fellow of Britain's Royal Aeronautical Society, but Mulally was not embarrassed about his role in charging up his team to do great things. After the plane was built, no one at Boeing could say exactly what Alan Mulally had contributed in terms of technical input during the four-year, $4 billion effort that produced the 777. But all the folks one talks with in Seattle give him full credit for inspiring *them* to produce a plane that *they* are all proud of. As one hard-nosed engineer explained to me, "Alan energized us."

Resource: *Robert E. Rosen, *Leading People* (New York: Viking Penguin, 1966).

Engaging the Middle

The mind likes a strange idea as little as the body likes a strange protein and resists it with similar energy. It would not perhaps be too fanciful to say that a new idea is the most quickly acting antigen known to science. If we watch ourselves honestly we shall often find that we have begun to argue against a new idea even before it has been completely stated.
—Wilfred Trotter

G reat minds are as one in concluding that groups resist change with all the vigor of antibodies attacking an intruding virus—but at least thirty-five reasonable theories have been adduced by scholars and philosophers to explain the source of that ubiquitous and inevitable resistance! In today's modern organizations, perhaps the most potent of those sources of resistance is the negative, reflexive response elicited in us all when someone tries to impose his or her will on us. Even when that person has legitimate authority to tell us what to do—and even when what we are asked to do is in our self-interest—we nonetheless bristle at the command.

Here's a testable proposition. Go up to a smoker and tell him or her, "Quit smoking! No excuses, now, you know it isn't good for you. So just do as I say, and stop." Not only won't that approach work, but you are likely to make an enemy and, perhaps, be told to "bug off." The reason for the negative reaction is that no one today is seen as having the right to impose his or her will on another adult. To do so is widely considered the ultimate act of disrespect for the rights and dignity of individuals. So try telling people not to smoke, and the predictable effect will be to heighten their desire to smoke (if only to spite you). They will ask, "Who the hell do you think you are to tell me how to live my life?"

In the individualistic, libertarian West the era has passed when dictators, kings, and even traditional bosses have the absolute right to tell us to do anything, let alone change a pattern of behavior with which we are comfortable. We, all of us, will rule ourselves these days. At the least, we feel entitled to a say in deciding how to deal with the problems that affect us directly.

In the early 1980s, when Jan Carlzon introduced a massive program to change the culture of SAS, he didn't get resistance from his top management team. After all, they had a say in designing the effort, and the changes involved no skin off their knees. Similarly, people on the front line embraced the proposed changes because they would become empowered to do what they knew would make their jobs more satisfying—namely, serve customers.

With that kind of support, Carlzon felt confident that he could quickly turn the ailing airline around. Yet, a year after the program was launched, he discovered that little in fact had changed and that all the efforts to enable SAS's customer-service reps to satisfy the needs of business customers had had little effect.

Carlzon discovered that the bottleneck was people in the middle of the organization—the managers and supervisors whose jobs traditionally had been to enforce the rules that top management now was jettisoning in favor of employee self-management. Without rules to enforce, SAS's middle managers didn't have a role to play. So they made work for themselves by preventing front-line employees from exercising initiative (or, in their view, from "running wild and acting without permission").

To overcome the paralyzing resistance of those in the middle, SAS's top management had to go back to square one, working with supervisors to redefine their role. It turned out that their traditional function of enforcing rules hadn't really been all that satisfying (who wants to be thought of as a cop?). Once SAS's supervisors understood that the proposed changes could entail their acting as *authorities* (expert consultants to workers and champions of those on the front line who needed resources from above) instead of *authoritarians* (mindless enforcers of bureaucratic rules), they saw that it was in their self-interest to get on board. Resistance then vanished, and the overall change effort finally started to work as intended.

Carlzon was a brilliant master of change, but even he neglected to ask himself the fundamental question all leaders must ask, and then answer: *What do I have to do to overcome my followers' resistance to change?*

Because change cannot be commanded—leaders cannot successfully impose their wills on followers—overcoming resistance entails enlisting others to willingly engage in the process. In the final analysis, people will only follow leaders who take them where they want to go. Leaders thus create followers by allowing them to take a leader's vision as their own because it is their own. Resistance is overcome when followers see that change is not only in their self-interest but that *they* are leading it.

Resource: *James O'Toole, "Change Resisted: Thirty-Three Hypotheses Why," in *Leading Change* (San Francisco: Jossey-Bass, 1995).

Expectations, Management of

I f you are looking for a fast and painless course on how a great leader mobilizes followers, run out to Blockbuster and rent the video of the 1982 Academy Award–winning film *Gandhi*. There's one scene, in particular, that tells you all you will ever need to know about managing expectations. We see Gandhi in 1917 visiting a remote Indian village beset by terrible famine and poverty (indirectly caused by the careless actions of British landlords). A village elder asks Gandhi for help. The Mahatma answers, "We shall do what we can do."

Wait a minute, that's not what political leaders are supposed to say! Certainly a U.S. politician would reply, "Vote for me, and I'll solve all your problems." The American way is for leaders to promise a (free-range) chicken in every pot, a Beemer in every garage—and the garage attached to a $2.5 mil fixer-upper in Aspen. Of course, they never deliver. And we respond by trusting 'em as far as we can throw 'em.

But listen to Gandhi. Note that he says "we" and not "I." He wants it known that he can't deliver anything by himself; *they* must all work together to solve their problems. And while he commits to action—to *do* something—even in so doing he lowers expectations appropriately. Realistically, he knows—and, importantly, the villagers also know—that the Brits are not going to leave India next week—or next year (in fact, it took another thirty years). And he can't guarantee them full bellies either. Yet because he respects the villagers enough to tell them the truth, they, in turn, place their trust in him—and then become his followers.

And you don't have to be Gandhian to make this work. France's Prime Minister Lionel Jospin faced his first real crisis when Air France's pilots went on strike just prior to the kickoff of the World Cup in France. Based on the past performance of Socialist prime ministers, the press (and the union) predicted that Jospin would intervene and then cave in to union demands. Instead, he insisted that the union negotiate directly with the head of Air France (and the strike was settled in time to play football). As one knowledgeable French observer explained to *Time* magazine, "That's Jospin's strength. He doesn't promise a lot, he just says, 'I'll do what I can.'" Jospin's predilection to commit only to what is doable and deliverable has generated widespread personal credibility and support for his government.

That's a perfect example of why leadership is an art and not a science. On the one hand, to be effective, leaders must issue real challenges to their people, must put out worthy goals that both engage them and stretch them. On the other hand, to be credible, leaders must not promise the moon, build unrealizable expectations, or set the bar so high as to discourage all effort. The trick is drawing the right line between the unmotivating extremes.

In business situations, the management of expectations is particularly tricky. If leaders promise too much, followers will be disappointed when they don't deliver, and trust will be destroyed; but if leaders hold out the prospect of achieving too little, followers will not be inspired to act, to change, or to follow. This is practical stuff with bottom-line implications. A while ago, I moderated a week-long session designed to produce strategic alignment among the top management team at a Fortune 500 company. During the week, the CEO announced that his goal was to generate something like a 20 percent annual increase in the stock price over the next five years and that he would pledge to do so at a forthcoming meeting with stock analysts.

When I suggested that it was rather risky to go out on that particular limb, the CEO turned red-faced and told me that I didn't understand the expectations of The Street. "Didn't Jack Welch go out on a limb when *he* promised to be #1 or #2 in every one of GE's businesses?" he shot back. Well, yes, but Welch had the power to deliver on that promise: he could sell off the #3s. In contrast, no CEO has enough control over market forces to promise a specific stock price—or even a rate of return that few mature companies have ever achieved or maintained. The CEO was right, of course (you can fool a lot of people—once). So, like lots of other greedy investors, I bought stock in the company . . . and then watched the bottom fall out over the next year, when returns were no better than average.

A nice thing about leadership is that it all comes down to common sense. Yet CEO after CEO makes the same knuckleheaded mistake of promising what he or she is unlikely to be able to deliver. Where this error is most evident is in new-company startups and IPOs, as I painfully learned while being a participant-observer in three such launches of promising enterprises. Regrettably, in all three instances the overenthusiasm of investment bankers and underwriters overcame the better judgment of company leaders—with the result that the company prospectuses all read like descriptions of Microsoft. Each of the companies extrapolated rates of growth for the first three years that would have made investors as rich as Bill Gates (or at least Warren Buffett). In fact, the first year's performance of each of those companies was pretty darn good. But the overhyped expectations of investors weren't met, and disinvestment followed swiftly on the heels of disappointment.

Setting appropriate expectations requires a delicate balance. But a useful rule of thumb in all leadership situations is to *underpromise and overdeliver*. Then, when followers, investors, and customers are dutifully impressed by your performance, it never hurts to underpromise again.

Resource: *Time,* October 12, 1998, p. 43.

LEADERSHIP
A to Z

Fear and Failure

Leadership requires uncommonly deep reservoirs of courage. Leaders put themselves at risk in every which way—emotionally, psychologically, socially, politically, economically, and, occasionally, even physically. Beginning with Jesus Christ, the catalogue of great leaders who paid the ultimate price includes Joan of Arc, Lincoln, Gandhi, Martin Luther King, Jr., Anwar Sadat, and John F. Kennedy.

A less dramatic fate—but a far more frequent one in all cultures and in all eras—has been *character assassination,* the all-too-common reward for leaders who seek to bring about fundamental change. At the end of his career, George Washington wrote to Thomas Jefferson that "every act of my administration [had been characterized] in such exaggerated and indecent terms as could scarcely be applied to a Nero, a notorious defaulter, or even a common pickpocket." And that's still the case today for leaders in such relatively nonviolent endeavors as business, academia, and the nonprofit sector. Even if the organization is a school or the Girl Scouts, it takes great courage to lead if you care at all about what people say about you.

The enemy of courage is fear. And most fears of leaders are hard to shake because they have strong anchors in reality. It is perfectly reasonable, after all, for U.S. presidents to fear for their personal safety. Likewise, it is reasonable for all leaders to fear that they will be unpopular when they propose change. Tina Brown made numerous enemies at *The New Yorker* when she deviated from the magazine's hallowed traditions. But she was willing to pay the price of unpopularity: she had the leader's courage to stare 'em in the eye and move ahead.

In the 1980s, Rene McPherson, who had been an extraordinarily successful CEO of the Dana Corporation, found himself in a situation akin to Brown's when, as an outsider, he was appointed to lead an inwardly focused organization. Sadly, his results were not as salubrious as Brown's, and, worse, his experience was far more typical of what most leaders encounter. When McPherson was named dean of Stanford's business school, the immediate reaction of the faculty was to dig in, pull their wagons in a circle, and fight every initiative he offered.

McPherson had arrived in Palo Alto with a well-deserved reputation as an advocate of progressive organizational practices; alas, change was the *last* thing on the faculty's agenda. During his brief tenure, the faculty made McPherson's life hell, seriously imperiling his health in the process. The lesson of McPherson's failure quickly spread to would-be academic administrators across this fair land: *beware, change equals suicide*. Thus did fear of the faculty replace the fear of God as utmost in the minds of B-School deans! (See Followership.)

Yet, in truth, the most common source of fear is the possibility of failure. Even more so than Shakespeare's bugaboo, conscience, it is fear of failure that "doth make cowards of us all." Because observation teaches us that most leaders who attempt to change things will fail, the risk-averse majority of leaders retreats to the safe haven of timidity. "Nothing ventured, nothing risked" is the unspoken motto of most administrators and managers.

Moreover, fear of failure becomes a self-fulfilling prophecy. Warren Bennis and Burt Nanus tell the story of the famous high-wire aerialist Karl Wallenda, who, throughout his long career, had successfully walked tightropes across some of the world's most dizzying chasms and abysses. When he fell to his death in 1978, his wife—also a renowned tightrope walker—was asked by reporters what she thought had gone wrong. She explained that her courageous husband had concentrated for decades on "walking the rope." He had been so self-confident, in fact, that he never thought of failure; the thought of falling had never even crossed his mind. But then, prior to his last, fateful walk, something had changed in his previously positive, optimistic, can-do attitude: All he could think about was the prospect of *falling*. Mrs. Wallenda explained that "it was the first time he had ever thought about that, and it seemed to me that he put all his energies into *not falling* rather than walking the tightrope."

Bennis and Nanus concluded that "the most impressive and memorable quality of the leaders we studied was the way . . . these leaders put all their energies into their task. They simply don't think about failure." Indeed, if leaders focus on the downside and the risks of their tasks, that will increase their already lousy odds against success. So instead of worrying about failure, leaders concentrate on running the gauntlet, walking the tightrope, and overlooking the risks inherent to all acts of true leadership. In sum, the "Wallenda factor" is a willingness to pay the price if things go awry. That's another way of saying that *leadership takes guts*.

Resources: *Warren Bennis and Burt Nanus, *Leaders* (New York: HarperCollins, 1985).
*Warren Bennis, *On Becoming a Leader* (Reading, Mass.: Addison-Wesley, 1989).

Focus

I f everyone had the same values, held the same things dear, shared the same objectives, and had the same interests, there would be no need for leadership. If we all wanted the same things, we simply would march together in unison without need of anyone to motivate us, guide us, or help us reach our common destination.

Alas, the real world is characterized instead by disagreements about ends, by competing self-interests, and by mutually incompatible values. Indeed, the sources of division and disagreement in nations and organizations are so numerous that there is always plenty of work for leaders to do! And the starting point for effective leadership is the conscious recognition of the basic and profound differences that exist among followers. Leaders must both appreciate that followers have legitimate differences and, at the same time, transcend those differences by identifying a common end that all parties will view as desirable.

Early in this century, Gandhi saw that the goal of independence from Britain could unite India's Moslems and Hindus who, on other matters, were very much at odds. In the late 1940s, Jean Monnet, the father of the European Common Market, saw that the desire for economic prosperity could transcend the nationalism that had long divided the warring tribes of Europe. And, in the 1980s, the leaders of the Ford Motor Company saw that a concern for "quality" could bridge the multifaceted differences that had for years stymied cooperation between the unions and management, line and staff, marketing and finance, and engineering and operations. That's why Gandhi focused all his energy on independence, Monnet focused entirely on economic cooperation, and Ford made quality "Job One."

A major challenge of leadership is to identify—or create—common ground where the diverse interests of followers can be made to overlap. Then, leaders must remain unremittingly focused on that shared territory, constantly reminding followers what their common objective is and why it is of overarching importance to *them*. By keeping the attention of everyone so focused, and their energy and effort tightly channeled, it becomes possible to avoid unproductive activities and to make potentially divisive concerns recede from prominence. At worst, followers will be so busy that they won't have time to brood about their pet projects and prejudices; at best, they will forget why it was they ever had disagreed!

Followership

By definition, leadership requires followership. Given Americans' enthusiasm for leadership, it must be noted that we lack concomitant passion for being followers. In a nation of rugged individualists, precious few desire the role of follower (indeed, in the extreme case of university faculties, the trait of followership is totally absent!). Nonetheless, despite its obvious value and virtue, the role and function of followership is generally misinterpreted.

For instance, in 1998 the CEO of a high-tech Silicon Valley firm berated his hundred top managers for their "lack of followership." Their perceived sin: they had given him the "candid feedback" he had requested (in a 360° evaluation of the company's leadership team), and he didn't like what he had heard. Reading between the lines, it was apparent to the CEO that his people saw him as an arrogant bully who was more interested in how he was personally portrayed in the business press than he was in leading them by providing a clear vision, consistent performance metrics, and so forth. In the most remarkable display of whining that I ever have had the embarrassment to witness, the CEO said that he would teach them all "a lesson" by not interacting with them again until they had demonstrated appropriate "obedience and loyalty."

I had signed a standard "confidentiality agreement," in which I swore not to reveal any of the company's strategic or technological secrets that I might pick up while attending the meeting. Well, I didn't hear a thing about such matters (and I wouldn't tell you if I did). Ironically, what I did learn was that the company's best kept dirty little secret was that the well-cultivated public persona of their cover-boy CEO was belied by reality. Over coffee, I sidled over to a manager who was standing alone and asked (as diplomatically as possible) what the motivation was for working at the company, given the abusive behavior of the CEO. Candidly, the executive told me, "We've got a strong technological advantage here, and it translates into fantastic pay and benefits." (See Comparative Advantage.)

So as long as the company keeps its technological edge—and its stock price high—I guess it doesn't matter that it lacks the kind of leadership needed when innovation and motivation are required for success. If you've discovered a gold mine, who needs followers? However, most of us don't work for companies that have been lucky enough to strike gold. In our workplaces, the attitude, loyalty, and behavior of followers is important to the success of the enterprise. And the point is, *such followership must be earned by leaders*. In order to identify what is required to attract followers, effective leaders begin by imagining themselves in the shoes of their constituents.

To this end, a particularly imaginative group of managers met at the University of Cape Town and composed the Followers Creed reproduced below. To my mind, this list of what followers require of leaders has the ring of universal validity:

I WILL FOLLOW YOU, IF YOU

- Treat me with respect
- Inspire me with your vision
- Teach me
- Are tolerant of my mistakes
- Are visible and available
- Talk with (and listen to) me
- Allow me to grow
- Don't give up, or change course arbitrarily
- Have the courage of your convictions
- Tell me the truth, and practice what you preach

For further evidence that this is what followers expect of leaders, please refer to the solid data cited in the resource below.

Resource: *James M. Kouzes and Barry Z. Posner, *The Leadership Challenge* (San Francisco: Jossey-Bass, 1997).

G

LEADERSHIP
A to Z

Generosity

BB has had two CEOs, Percy Barnevik and Goran Lindahl, since its creation on January 1, 1988. Those two relatively unassuming Swedes created an extraordinary company by seriously studying the best organizational practices, most innovative policies, and most farsighted business experiments (successes *and* failures) in Europe, the United States, and Asia over the previous twenty years. Then, they analyzed what they found—sifting, sorting, evaluating, and examining the lessons from various perspectives—and applied the core learnings from hundreds of organizations in a boldly original way. The most powerful idea they appropriated was the notion of cascading leadership; through its application thousands of engineers and managers down through ABB's ranks were developed into effective leaders of the organization. (See **A**BB's Benchstrength.)

Besides their uncommon openness and capacity to learn from others, what the Swedes brought to ABB's organizational admixture of spare parts, ready-mades, and the prematurely abandoned ideas of others was one peculiar, and previously untested, leadership value. In selecting its potential leaders, ABB—like many other progressive companies—looks for men and women who have experience, flexibility, and integrity. But ABB is unique in that it also requires the quality of *generosity*. No, that isn't a typo, or a mistranslation from the Swedish: CEO Lindahl says that ABB needs generous leaders in order to realize its goal of becoming a self-driven, self-renewing organization.

What does ABB mean by generosity? In Swedish, as well as in English, generosity entails "liberality in giving." Generous leaders give their time willingly and unselfishly to their colleagues. Of course, it is not time, per se, that peers and subordinates look to their leaders to give; rather, they seek the things that take time to give, such as the benefit of the leader's experience, knowledge, contacts, information, advice, and counsel. Generous leaders also give praise, credit, and encouragement. Most important, they are willing to give up the very currency of organizational power—turf, budgets, staff, territory, titles (even corner offices)—when doing so enhances the greater good of the corporation.

And no, ABB's Barnevik and Lindahl are not utopians, idealists, or fools. In fact, they are clear-eyed realists who understand that such generosity is "unnatural" in large organizations and that one giver would be taken advantage of among a pack of power-hungry takers. Hence, they have created the conditions under which generosity is *institutionalized:* they reward it. At ABB, leaders don't get promoted who aren't generous; they don't get bonuses for beggaring their peers; and they don't get ahead, period, if they aren't routinely observed giving, sharing, and helping others—and that's the rule, even for executives who are making their numbers in a big way. (See Controls.)

This is not an exercise in altruism. It is all very practical, given ABB's goal of creating a self-driven, self-renewing company. The opposite, of course, is a reactive, static organization. Such companies helplessly lurch from crisis to crisis, caught in a cycle of complacent self-satisfaction and then—as the world inevitably changes—panic, followed by painful restructuring, reengineering, and downsizing (as at General Motors, for example).

The spirit of generosity is seen as a necessity at ABB because it is the vital fluid that nourishes the teamwork, cooperation, collaboration, alignment, and shared learning needed in a self-renewing organization. Barnevik and Lindahl know that selfish leaders aren't team players and that the noble objective of learning is unattainable in an organization where people won't willingly teach others what they have learned.

Here's a practical test of generosity: at ABB, when a leader of one of its nearly five thousand profit centers encounters serious problems making his or her numbers, peers from around the world will willingly drop what they are doing to lend a hand. Try it in your own organization. Will managers—who are competing with each other for bonuses, promotions, and praise—selflessly act to help a peer who is in trouble? If that's the cultural norm, congratulations! Your organization, like ABB, is characterized by generosity! If it isn't, invest your retirement savings in another company, and then ask yourself, "What the hell am I doing working here?"

Better still, figure out what *you* have to do to get others to become generous. That's what leaders do.

Getting Started

hen Lew Platt became CEO of Hewlett-Packard in 1992, he was only the third person in the company's history to hold that title. He was an experienced executive, he had worked at H-P for twenty-six years, and because he had been for some time the designated successor to CEO John Young, he had had plenty of time to prepare himself for the challenges of leadership. Given all that experience and preparation, he nonetheless was faced with the same fundamental question every new leader must answer: *Where do I start?* Here's what he did:

1. *He established a leadership team.* In selecting the team, he sent a signal to the organization about his priorities, goals, and agenda. Because being chosen for the top management team was an important step in the firm's succession planning, Platt was careful to pick people who supported the values that he deemed critical for the ongoing success of the company. He looked not only for people who were compatible team players but also for people who

117

represented a diversity of perspectives. (Platt, a candid leader who admits his own mistakes, in hindsight acknowledges that he picked one outsider who couldn't adapt to the team and that he took too long to correct the mistake.) Platt also had spent time learning what he didn't know and, hence, was able to recruit a team that compensated for his weaknesses: "I am not a brilliant strategist, but I know one when I see one. I have to surround myself with people who can help me to think strategically."

2. *He listened and set an agenda.* While preparing to assume leadership, Platt spent many hours "walking around" in the H-P tradition, listening to the needs, concerns, and aspirations of employees, managers, and customers. He thus took office with an agenda of three major issues that needed to be addressed: revitalizing the "H-P Way" (the company's unique culture of innovation and decentralization that had not received adequate attention in recent years); restoring the company's historically stable financial performance (it had been more like a roller-coaster ride during the previous few years); and reframing the strategy (to focus on emerging challenges three or four years in the future). His major long-term concerns were the challenges of revitalization and continual growth: "Nobody stays on top forever. Sears had both what Wal-Mart has *and* the catalog business, but still fell down. IBM started telling customers what they needed instead of listening to customers. Since H-P has moved from a challenger to a leader, the thing that worries me most is complacency. How do you maintain the

edge? We have great people and talent, they are motivated, and we need to ensure that they stay that way."

3. *He built the case for change.* Platt spent only 25 percent of his time on operations. The other three-quarters he devoted to communicating the need for breakthrough performance in the key areas on his agenda. He accomplished this by going on the road and talking directly with H-P people in operations around the globe. He challenged them to perform at higher levels, even as he restored pride in H-P's principles and values. Because one of those key values is decentralization, he pushed responsibility for change down to operational levels and held the appropriate people accountable for realizing the needed changes.

4. *He concentrated on what only he could do as CEO.* Platt was not spending his time on operations, so he was able to spend more time dealing with H-P's key constituencies. He reached out to customers, opened effective channels of communications with the H-P board, and, of course, spent more time listening to employees at all levels and communicating repeatedly the importance of items 2 and 3 above. (See **U**p and Out.)

Today, H-P is facing a new set of challenges. Will Platt be as up to meeting them as he was up to the twin strategic leadership tasks of alignment and adaptability when he first became CEO? (See **M**uddled Teams.) As Yogi Berra said, "It ain't over 'til it's over."

Globalism

It has now become a commonplace that leaders of global corporations must respond to the needs of local markets while, at the same time, adhering to the same management principles and core values in all their operations around the world. But it was in the early 1960s when Sony's Akio Morita became the first CEO to teach his people to *think globally, act locally*. Like Morita, the leaders of such truly global corporations as ABB, Nestle, IBM, and CALTEX now routinely pay close attention to local customs and cultures, while never losing sight of the fact that certain management practices are universal and that treating all customers and employees around the world with equal respect is the bottom line of globalism.

Even though that much is understood, there is, unfortunately, a widely held misperception that there is also a unique body of knowledge, a distinct discipline, entitled "global leadership." Indeed, many would-be leaders believe there is a distinct "U.S. leadership," "Belgian leadership," "Cantonese leadership," and so on through the gazetteer! This misunderstanding grows quite naturally out of the obvious fact that laws and customs differ—often markedly—from nation to nation (and even within such multicultural nations as India).

For example, Chinese employees expect a Lunar New Year bonus from employers that is equal to a month's pay; wearing Bermuda shorts in the Japanese subsidiary of a U.S. high-tech firm is always a no-no (even if you can get away with it back at your Silicon Valley headquarters); and as Disney learned the hard way, employers in France don't tell employees how long to wear their hair or what constitutes "proper" grooming. Similarly, consumer preferences vary from country to country: U.S. soft drink companies learned long ago that upping their sugar content works wonders in many markets in the developing world; auto makers know that big cars are a tough sell in countries with crowded streets and high gas prices; and Disney (again) learned that the French like a little wine with lunch, even at amusement parks.

Such significant cultural differences notwithstanding, *good leadership is good leadership everywhere.* A visit to any of IKEA's 142 stores in twenty-nine countries around the world is a good place to gain an understanding of what global leadership really means in practice. IKEA's furniture and its concepts of space management vary widely from country to country—but its philosophy, values, principles, and unique Scandinavian "style" are the same everywhere. IKEA's mission, to offer "a wide range of home furnishing items of good design and function, at prices so low that the majority of people can afford to buy them," is the same whether it is operating "at home" in Scandinavia or in Taiwan or Saudi Arabia. Even the unique Scandinavian product image—simplicity in design and clean lines—is not modified for Asian or Arabian markets.

What differs from country to country are such things as the size of products (Americans like big beds), unique national products (the French prefer armoires to closets), and the layout of stores (Asians don't mind cramped spaces that would make

Americans claustrophobic). And, of course, the French expect to find a choice of fine wines in IKEA lunchrooms. But IKEA's basic business model is the same everywhere: the company has a unique set of competencies, including Scandinavian design, strategic sourcing, vertical integration, attractive stores, low prices, and distinctive imaging, that allow it to deliver on its mission the world over.

In its management practices, IKEA obeys the labor laws of each country in which it operates and customizes its employee relations where necessary (for example, the disciplined Germans like precise procedures and the French demand formal job descriptions). Yet, when it comes to the heart of IKEA's management philosophy— the leadership values of openness, egalitarianism, informality, consensus-based decision making, "learning by doing," and sharing information at all levels—the organization's culture transcends all national boundaries. Those core principles and beliefs are clearly enunciated in founder Ingvar Kamprad's "Testament," which has been translated into the dozen languages spoken by IKEA employees and is the focus of the firm's regularly conducted global leadership seminars.

It has been suggested that IKEA's culture—like ABB's, SAS's, and Ericsson's—is "uniquely Swedish." In fact, the leaders of those companies, along with hundreds of other Swedish managers, academics, and union leaders, spent much of the 1960s and 1970s studying the best leadership principles from around the world, seeking to discover universal values and practices that work everywhere. They found that the common denominator is treating people with respect and dignity, and there is nothing uniquely Swedish about that.

Sadly, those who stress cultural differences in leadership practices and principles—"Asian values" and the like—often cloak mistreatment of workers in Third World countries in the language of cultural sensitivity. For example, Nike was big on respecting Asian customs. And even the enlightened leaders of Motorola didn't include their Asian employees in their vaunted participative-management program in the 1980s, although they claimed the program was at the heart of their culture and success. Cutting their Asian workers out of the company's bonus system was justified in terms of sensitivity to local customs.

Don't be fooled by those who masquerade as culturally enlightened. With only a few exceptions, the things leaders do that are described in these pages are applicable around the world, as the practices of such truly global corporations as Sony and IKEA demonstrate. Doubtless, being sensitive to local customs, on the one hand, and treating people everywhere with equal dignity, on the other, is a difficult balance to maintain—but that is the essence of "global" leadership. Remember, the only thing worse than a boorish manager who is insensitive to foreign customs and cultures is a P.C. manager who is convinced that everything everywhere is so different that treating people the world around with equal respect is Eurocentrism!

Resource: *Paul Grol and Christopher Schoch, *IKEA,* Report 6541 (Paris: Paris Chamber of Commerce and Industry, 1997).

Grandstanding

The infamous 1963 tableau lingers in the collective memory: Governor George Wallace standing defiantly in the doorway of the University of Alabama. When Wallace died in 1998, commentators recalled that not only had he been doing the wrong thing morally but he had been grandstanding to boot! In effect, he had been *posing* as a leader because he never had any intention of trying to stop the first black students from enrolling. He had known full well that desegregation was a *fait accompli*. His posturing had been a photo op cynically designed to advance his political aspirations. Once his picture had been snapped, he quietly stepped out of the way of U.S. Justice Department officials and National Guard troops, as scripted.

Ineffectual leaders attempt to manipulate perceptions in order to give the appearance of leadership. Whereas true leaders devote their energies to important tasks that address the true needs of followers, the concern of impostors is with their personal agendas and not with the real work of leadership.

In the corporate arena, the behavior of ineffectual leaders is seldom as cynical (or immoral) as that of politicians. Nonetheless, there are temptations for them to grandstand as well, the most obvious of which is there in neon lights: *MERGE*. CEOs who run out of ideas, who don't have a clue how to stimulate internal growth or innovation, and who don't have the ambition, energy, or courage to lead true transformations of their organizations often are unable to resist the juiciest temptation to be proffered since the Edenic apple.

When all else fails, CEOs predictably go to a Wall Street yenta to arrange a match with a similarly lonesome CEO. We know the script by heart: the love-besotted duo woo, propose an exchange of vows, and then celebrate their blessed union with public nuptials (a.k.a. a press conference). Because the Wall Street crowd always cries at weddings, the newly joined CEOs can relax in the knowledge that nothing more will be expected of them in terms of results until death (read retirement) doth them part.

Never mind that the old M & A gambit seldom generates enough real, long-term growth to cover the cost of the reception. True, there have been a few arranged, midlife corporate marriages that have been long and happy (CALTEX, FujiXerox, OwensCorning), but most don't last as long as a Hollywood romance (witness AT&T and NCR, Du Pont and Conoco). Conglomerate marriages from disparate industries are particularly rocky—RJR and Nabisco never discovered an ounce of blissful synergy, and whatever happened to ITT or "Engulf and Devour" (Gulf+Western)? Even marriages within the same industry often lead to broken hearts (Bank of America learned there is no such thing as a marriage of true minds in the business world—"merger" was the euphemism that the predatory NationsBank used as cover for what was a blatant rape of the venerable B of A).

And who benefits from these highly publicized amalgamations of giant organizations: long-term investors? customers? employees? communities? As the French say, *phut!* The beneficiaries are the Wall Street firms who broker and finance the deals, short-term stock speculators, and, of course, the good ol' CEOs who mastermind these gems of legerdemain—and are off to Tucson before long-term stockholders catch onto the fact they've been had (again).

Obviously, some megamergers make sense (the Chrysler/Daimler-Benz match shows signs of working), and the acquisition of small companies by large ones is a necessary source of capital (and a well-earned payoff) for inventors and entrepreneurs. But, in a great number of instances, strategic alliances are a more effective and appropriate alternative if, in fact, the motivating force is performance and not grandstanding. In sum, most megamergers between giant firms are little more than substitutes for true, transformational leadership.

One final note about George Wallace. At the end of his career, he surprised the world by atoning for his immoral behavior. As an old man, he visited an African-American church, admitted his sins, and asked for the parishioners' forgiveness. Christians say the act saved his soul; it certainly earned him respect even from his enemies. How many leaders in the public or private sectors have the insight to recognize their errors and the courage and decency to admit their mistakes publicly? At the end, George Wallace actually may have become a true leader.

———————

Resource: *John R. Harbison and Peter Pekar, *Smart Alliances* (San Francisco: Jossey-Bass, 1998).

Guvmint Work

On the theory that "if you can make it there, you can make it anywhere," let's review a couple of examples of effective leadership in the most unlikely of venues: Washington, D.C. Conventional Wisdom (CW) has it that government bureaucracies exist to serve the bureaucrats who inhabit them and that those calcified organizations have ironclad resistance mechanisms that make them immune to the contaminating virus of change. Well, CW hasn't visited the Department of Veterans Affairs lately—an organization that, until 1998, had a secure niche among the capital's top ten most arrogant, unresponsive, and ossified bureaucracies. There, Undersecretary for Benefits Joe Thompson has infected his agency with a sincere desire to serve its clientele and has changed employee behavior accordingly.

Thompson's Olympian leadership of change at the Veterans Benefits Administration not only matches, but exceeds, the best private sector experience in both degree of difficulty and execution. Although the VBA's cultural transformation deserves an entire volume dedicated to describing what Thompson did, how he did it, and how leaders in the public and private sectors can learn from his example, here's the short of it:

- Thompson engaged the VBA's key stakeholders in creating a shared sense of what the organization could become, its potential for serving with honor the men and women who served all Americans. In particular, he created conditions under which employees could identify a rewarding role for themselves in realizing this morally superior vision for the VBA. (See **V**ision.)
- Thompson created the conditions under which VBA employees could discover for themselves what behavior was required of them, and he provided the opportunity for them to acquire the skills and tools they needed to do the right things.
- Thompson provided incentives for his people to behave in ways consistent with the new mission, vision, and values of the VBA, and then he got out of the way and let them lead (all the while protecting them from retro forces on high in the Administration and the Congress).

Here are just two examples of what he did to accomplish this. First, he demonstrated his personal commitment to leading the change. Early on, Thompson spent a full week cloistered with his hundred top people, sleeves rolled up, jointly building the leadership skills they needed to cascade requisite changes down the organization. Second, even more unusual, he focused on the hard stuff of change. He encouraged VBA's leaders to spend months generating "balanced performance measures," a quantified scorecard that focuses the efforts of everyone on doing the things that matter and allows them continually to assess how they are performing in relation to their ultimate goal of providing excellent service.

As effectively as any organization I have studied, the VBA clearly identified what they were trying to achieve and then linked everything—structure, rewards, information, communication—to this vision.

Significantly, not only did behavior change at the VBA, but within a year their balanced-performance-measures approach was being replicated at the Internal Revenue Service. Although the IRS did not attempt as thorough a cultural change as the VBA, to its credit it was able to focus the efforts of its multitude of unionized workers on just four key metrics: quality and quantity of work, and customer and employee satisfaction. As a result, the causes of the IRS's well-deserved reputation for being an agency with an attitude were effectively addressed.

In essence, what Thompson (and the leaders of the IRS) did was to include everybody in their organizations in all aspects of their respective transformations—and then give them measures to assess how they were doing in meeting their objectives.

This effort brings to mind an instructive story that Booz·Allen & Hamilton's Paul Anderson tells about one of the first (nonconfrontational) military encounters between U.S. and Soviet forces that occurred shortly after the fall of the Berlin Wall. It seems that the commanders of U.S. and Soviet divisions were having a friendly chat over coffee when a Russian general confided that he had been shocked to learn that a U.S. tank driver had a map! "In the Red Army, you have to be at least a colonel before you can have a map."

Anderson points out that, in successful organizational transformations, leaders trust everyone down the line with a "map." This map is the vision of where the organization is headed and what behaviors are needed to get there. The VBA's balanced performance measures are key indicators of where people are on the map (that is, how far they are from their goal); and not only do all leaders down the line have the same map, but they are all taught how to read it, and all are authorized to use it. Joe Thompson—a military vet himself—knows that an organization in which only the top brass has access to relevant information is one that will get lost before it reaches its goal.

Then there's the Congress. In recent years, Capitol Hill has been even less fertile ground than the federal bureaucracy for the nurturing of leadership. Yet, like a hardy lichen thriving against all odds in the hostile Arctic tundra, Senator Tom Daschle's leadership has surprised his political friends and foes alike by bringing a semblance of unity to that most fractious of bodies, the Democratic Party caucus. The improbability of this feat should not be underestimated: Will Roger's famous quip "I am not a member of any organized party—I am a Democrat" is doubtless as accurate today as it was when he offered it more than sixty-five years ago.

When Daschle first stood for election to the post of Senate minority leader, his candidacy was opposed by none other than the dean of the chamber, Senator Robert C. Byrd, who argued that Daschle wasn't "tough enough for the job." Four years later, Byrd said, "I am here today to tell you that I was totally wrong" and that Daschle is "a man with steel in his spine despite his reasonable and modest demeanor."

What did Daschle do as a leader to unite his party and win over his critics? What is the source of his steely backbone? In a word, "inclusion—that has a lot to do with the cohesion we've been able to acquire," Daschle told *Los Angeles Times* reporter Edwin Chen. According to fellow Senators, Daschle listens intently to what they have to say, meeting with all his colleagues individually and in small groups, often spending as much as an hour on the phone with the particularly recalcitrant ones.

"He listens to everybody's points of view, and appears to be interested in what they say," according to Senator Bob Graham, "but he still has in the back of his mind a gyroscope that knows where he's trying to get to." Daschle is thus not prisoner to the opinions of his colleagues; instead, he listens to their concerns and ideas and then reframes them in ways that build consensus.

According to Senate Minority Whip Harry Reid, Daschle "doesn't freelance things. He has a leadership group. He runs ideas through them. If he has bad ideas they are dropped." His colleagues thus praise him for his loyalty to *them*: they say he makes them more effective by herding them and focusing *their* efforts. Thus, even among the hyperinflated egos on the Hill, leadership is recognized, respected, . . . and even rewarded: Daschle was initially elected to his post by the margin of a single vote; when he came up for reelection, he was chosen unanimously.

So what do we learn from our brief Washington visit? Although leading senators is different from leading bureaucrats, Tom Daschle and Joe Thompson nonetheless do several important things in common: they listen to where their followers want to go; they remove the obstacles that prevent them from achieving their aspirations; they keep them focused on important and measurable goals; and they include them in every step of the journey. A private sector leader could do worse than emulate this behavior (and, if you do copy it, I promise not to tell anyone where you learned these lessons).

Resource: Edwin Chen, "Daschle: Driving Force Behind Democrats' Power," *Los Angeles Times,* January 30, 1999, p. A12.

LEADERSHIP
A to Z

Hangings, Public

The downside and the dark side of leadership are common themes in Shakespeare's tragedies. In *Hamlet, King Lear, Othello,* and *Macbeth,* the playwright exposes the traps that frequently ensnare unwitting leaders, even as he explores how their own behavior leads to their downfall. From the tragedies we learn about the perils of indecision, about the dangerous allure of power, and about the self-destructive nature of pride, envy, denial, and anger.

In a few of the Bard's histories, he gets around to illuminating some of the positive aspects of leadership. But only in *Henry V* does Shakespeare treat the subject in a consistently bright light. The test of Henry's leadership comes when his friend of yore, Bardolph, is caught looting a church while serving in France as a foot soldier in the king's expeditionary army. In order to demonstrate his commitment to military discipline, Henry refuses to stay the order of Bardolph's execution. Henry thus puts the consistent enforcement of his prohibition against abusing French civilians above the call of friendship.

Shakespeare shows that public hangings—when used sparingly and with a clear purpose to instruct—can be a powerful tool in the hands of a virtuous leader. Today's figurative equivalent of hanging is, of course, the firing or dismissal of managers who violate important organizational norms. When corporate leaders sack supervisors who have abused workers, when they dismiss managers who have embezzled or bribed, and when they force resignations of key executives whose behavior blatantly belies stated organizational values, they send powerful messages throughout employee ranks. Indeed, it is an abdication of leadership responsibility to fail to punish those who defy an organization's basic standards of behavior. Yet because the message inherent in a "hanging" is so powerful, the risk is that it will be diluted by overuse. Moreover, firings must be used selectively for appropriately grave offenses and only in instances where the desired lesson will be unambiguously grasped by all.

Let it be noted that Shakespeare was ambivalent about one instance in which Henry decided to make an example of a misbehaving subject. In *Henry IV, Part II,* when the young Prince Hal is about to become King Henry, he has an opportunity to reprieve another old friend, Sir John Falstaff, who has committed a rather mundane offense. But rather than admit that he had once been the old man's partner in revelry and debauchery—and to set himself clearly above his subjects—Prince Hal pretends not to know Falstaff when the harmless old tub of lard names him as a character reference.

Although Henry had good instincts in not tolerating criminal behavior on the part of followers, Shakespeare makes us ask whether Henry's rather pedestrian purpose in permitting Falstaff's imprisonment is adequate justification for such self-serving and callous behavior toward a friend in a time of need. Moreover, all the people Henry chooses to make examples of are individuals of little political or economic consequence—that is, they are not the nobles and other high-placed individuals who seem immune to hanging, no matter how disreputable their behavior. At a minimum, Shakespeare implies that there may have been a double standard in Henry's England.

Here's the lesson: cowardly leaders fire offenders who are weak and insignificant; courageous leaders fire high-profile, powerful—and even productive—individuals who brazenly and defiantly choose to foul the organization's well.

Hierarchy

There is increasing consensus that hierarchical organizations commanded by single, all-powerful individuals are ill-equipped to cope with the emerging, fast-changing, knowledge economy. Ray Lane, president and COO of the Oracle Corporation, argues that "knowledge has become more important than tangible assets" in the new business environment. To succeed, corporations thus must become "networked" organizations in which the task of leaders is to oversee a "set of projects linked by similar intent." According to Lane, such organizations—like the best software firms today—are "less physical and less hierarchical" than the manufacturing giants of the past.

Michael Boxberger, CEO of Korn/Ferry International, cites a study sponsored by his firm that shows "creative collaboration is a key requirement for both the current and future corporate environment." The study found that "command and control" must give way to collaboration because "the scale of today's problems makes teamwork a necessity." Alas, Boxberger also notes that the study revealed today's leaders tend to cling to the old top-down model. Thus, "there is a disconnect between what is said and what is done."

The problem Boxberger cites is endemic. When people say "teamwork," CEOs invariably hear "anarchy." Even that certifiable sage Peter Drucker doesn't get it when he hears the likes of Lane and Boxberger advocate the necessity of "flattening" the organization: "To talk of the death of hierarchy is nonsense. In a crisis there has to be somebody who makes the final decision. If the ship goes down, the captain does not call a meeting. He gives an order."

With advice like that, it is no wonder Boxberger finds a disconnect between the actual behavior of CEOs and how they need to lead! The influential Drucker—perhaps because he cut his teeth at General Motors in the 1940s—reinforces the maladaptive behavior of his many readers by harkening back to Detroit's outmoded hierarchical model. But does this model square with reality? Is a company really like the Titanic? Do companies, in fact, suddenly—and without any warning—hit the business equivalent of icebergs? Try naming a company that went into crisis and sunk in the course of the same business day without there being opportunity for the CEO to consult with his top management team.

And hasn't Drucker misstated what Boxberger, Lane, and others are saying about hierarchy? Do those who advocate flatter structures *really* claim there shouldn't be a final authority in an organization? Max DePree, the former Herman Miller CEO who was an early proponent of giving all employees a voice, pointed out that an executive who listens to the wisdom of others isn't abdicating responsibility for the resulting decision: "Participative management guarantees that decisions will not be arbitrary, secret, or closed to questioning. Participative management is not democratic. Having a say differs from having a vote."

The problem with leaders who are given to command and control is that *every* problem is interpreted as a crisis, and every crisis is an excuse not to consult others before making "tough" decisions. That behavior is self-defeating. In the 99.9

percent of decisions that leaders confront in real life, there is plenty of time for the collaboration, teamwork, and consultation that lead not only to better and more informed decisions but to the buy-in needed for subsequent implementation. And if a real crisis were to occur, a team-oriented leader would have accumulated so much moral authority that followers wouldn't second-guess her if she were forced to make a solo decision to save the ship.

So I must respectfully disagree with what Peter Drucker says. To be effective, today's leaders must forgo the self-satisfaction that comes from playing Captain Bligh and learn the art of team leadership. One-man, hierarchical rule didn't work even in the eighteenth-century British navy—and corporate crews are a hell of a lot more mutinous today!

Resources: Glenn Rifkin, "Leadership in the Digital Age," Booz·Allen & Hamilton, 1998.
Industryweek, September 21, 1998, p. 104.
*Max DePree, *Leadership Is an Art* (New York: Dell, 1989).

Hope

Things are never as good as they ought to be, never as good as they could be, and everybody knows it. In a nation that is misgoverned, the citizens are aware of the evidence; and in a company that is mismanaged, the employees are aware of the telltale signs. But the lot of people in most misgoverned countries, and most mismanaged organizations, is that they must learn to live with their fate. Indeed, most learn to endure because they know from experience that "nothing ever changes."

The first challenge of leadership is not, as we are often told, to create a burning platform—most people, in fact, see their organization's problems. The real challenge is to lift them out of their state of resignation—a condition that masquerades as lethargy—and to help them embrace change. (See **R&R**.) Certainly, fear of losing their jobs will open their eyes . . . but only the prospect of redemption will motivate them to act positively.

India's masses remained sullenly acquiescent to British rule for generations, even though they had been exhorted to follow a parade of revolutionary terrorists and smarmy politicians who had promised to lead them against the obviously unjust British Raj. But it was only when Gandhi gave them *hope*—by showing them that he had an effective and moral strategy—that the people of India mobilized themselves to demand independence.

When Percy Barnevik assumed the leadership of ABB, he quickly got the attention of managers by showing them that the company was likely to lose the long-term struggle for markets against such powerhouse competitors as GE, Siemens, and Hitachi. But, in the final analysis, what prompted ABB's managers to shed their habitual somnolence—*and to actually change their behavior*—was Barnevik's argument that they had what it took to be great. What motivated the managers *to act* was Barnevik's graphic demonstration that if they capitalized on ABB's existing strengths, they could be the best corporation in their industry, and they finally could be *somebody* (not just a perpetual also-ran).

In 1630, the first governor of the Massachusetts Bay Colony, John Winthrop, inspired his early band of settlers with a prospect of what the New World might become: "We shall be as a city on the hill, the eyes of all people on us." Winthrop thus gave his followers a sense of hope that not only sustained them through the first life-threatening New England winter but also laid the basis for a dream that would energize many subsequent generations of Americans. *Hope:* it's the essence of "the vision thing."

How *Not* to Create Followers

The instructive article reproduced below is from the *Los Angeles Times*:

Health Chief Vows "Brutal" Shake-Up If Managers Resist Change
Los Angeles County health services chief Mark Finucane on Wednesday promised a "quick and unfortunately brutal shake-up" of his top managers who fail to help turn the embattled department around.

"I'm taking a hard look at everybody who reports to me, and I'm taking a hard look at the quality of work everybody does," Finucane told state legislators and Los Angeles County supervisors at a briefing on the continuing county health care crisis.

Finucane, who took over the troubled $2.3 billion Department of Health Services last month with orders from the supervisors to "change it as fast as you possibly can," said he has run into heavy resistance from some workers in the 25,000 member agency who "think I am a tourist."

But Finucane, who held a similar post in Contra Costa County for many years, insisted that he is "committed to change." He warned that any of the 50 or so top managers who did not join him and meet his high standards for performance could seek employment elsewhere.

"This is going to be a very, very quick and unfortunately brutal process," Finucane said. "There are significant reorganizations that I plan to present to the board."

Later, he told a reporter that "new rules" would be explained to the executives. He said be believes most will support the changes as the health care system shifts emphasis from traditional treatment at hospitals to less costly outpatient care at community clinics.

"You have to give them a chance to change," he said of the executives, most of whom are protected by Civil Service. "A lot of them are going to do so. Some can't."

He said those found lacking would be encouraged to offer their services elsewhere. To cut costs last year, about 2,600 department employees were terminated.

Here's a pop quiz: identify at least five things Mr. Finucane did that were likely to have increased resistance to change among the people he had just been appointed to lead. (Answers appear on the next page.)

1. He went public with criticisms of his people, insulting their intelligence and questioning both their ability and their commitment to the overall good of the institution.

2. He failed to include followers in the process of designing the change effort, thus making it difficult to get buy-in.

3. He threatened his people (instead of challenging them or appealing to their common interests).

4. He created an adversarial situation: the egotistical "I" (Finucane with all the answers) vs. "Them" (the clueless and benighted followers).

5. He created unreasonable expectations about time (nobody ever changed a bureaucracy overnight) and process (civil servants can't be dismissed on grounds of "resisting change").

6. [Extra credit for this answer] He caused his people to conclude he was a madman even before they had met him. Apparently, he had been so desperate for the job that he had failed to negotiate achievable performance objectives with the board that hired him. (See Up and Out.)

Resource: Carl Ingram, "Metro News," *Los Angeles Times,* February 22, 1996.

How to Create Followers

*I*nclusion. In a word, that's the secret to enlisting followers. Leaders create followers by including them in the process of change.

It's a verifiable proposition. You could test it by assigning your work team the task of developing a new operating plan for the group (or a new vision/ strategy/structure—it doesn't matter what, as long as it's an important task). Include everybody in the process who will be affected—*except one person*. Leave him or her out in the dark. Then, when the plan is complete, and everyone on the team is convinced that it is ready for implementation, call the excluded individual in and show him or her the great plan that the rest of you produced. "Well, Mary, what do you think of our plan?" you will ask, proud as punch of the fruits of your labor.

OK, you get the point. The excluded individual is probably going to criticize it, nit-pick it, find whatever fault she can with it—and, sure as hell, she isn't going to lift a finger to help in the implementation of *your* plan! Why? Not because there is anything intrinsically wrong with the plan, but because Mary was excluded from participating in its development. The simple act of exclusion sent a powerful message that the group didn't see her as significant enough to be included or as having anything worthwhile to contribute.

Exclusion is thus the ultimate expression of disrespect for an individual in an organizational context. Now, one might make light of this by calling it a mere case of "hurt feelings" or "oversensitivity" on the part of the excluded individual—but the impact on the organization can't be so easily dismissed. To see why, merely expand the experiment: multiply the number of excluded individuals, even leave out a whole department or a division. Now, try to get change implemented when there are large numbers of people who feel excluded from the process! That's the way it is in many large organizations.

Consider the consequences if you did the hypothetical experiment a different way, this time including everyone on your work team—even that ornery cuss who is always negative about everything. You know who, the one it is tempting to exclude because his sour attitude and knee-jerk opposition to all new ideas make it so hard to build consensus in favor of change. Yup, even include him in the experiment. Every time he objects to something, listen thoughtfully and respectfully, and give him honest reasons why when you are in disagreement. At the end of the process ask him, "What do you think of our plan?"

Now, let's be realistic. If he didn't get his way he is never going to be an enthusiastic supporter. But will he fight it, will he bad mouth it, will he resist its implementation? Most likely, he will reluctantly go along. Moreover, if he sees that everyone else is enthusiastic and working hard on implementation, and he then finds himself isolated, he will have two choices: either get on board or get out. Chances are, if the person has been shown respect by the group, he'll get with the drill.

The virtue of participatory management isn't that it leads to a utopia in which happy workers democratically arrive at a consensus on everything without conflict and without need of leadership. Hardly. Participation is simply the most practical (and moral) way to deal with the reality that not everyone in a group is going to agree about what needs to be done. Leaders can't impose their will on followers because that just gets their backs up. (See **E**ngaging the Middle.) It makes followers feel disrespected when leaders assume they have the right to tell them what to think and what to do. But leaders can turn resisters into followers by the simple act of including them in the process of change. Leaders understand that *if you respect followers, they will respect you.* (See **Z**enith.)

LEADERSHIP
A to Z

Inequality

All leaders are *not* created equal. Because not all people have equal ability, not everyone can be an Abe Lincoln, a Jack Welch, or a Margaret Thatcher. In fact, leadership talent and ability are as widely dispersed as the ability to play the piano or hit a curve ball. Moreover, 99 percent of us will never head a country, be CEO of a company, or lead any organization bigger or more powerful than the local PTA.

Nonetheless, every leader at every level can become better at the task through practice. All of us can get better at leadership by learning to do those things—and, in particular, to *focus* on those things—that determine effectiveness. And even if we are leading only one other person, we ought to have the appropriate ambition to lead him or her to the full extent of our given capabilities. If we don't work to be the best leaders we are each capable of becoming, we will harm our follower(s) and disappoint ourselves.

Intelligence

Here's a statement that is almost always false: *I don't have the brains to be a leader.* OK, so you don't have the fire power needed for genetic research, to fathom quarks, or even to solve Rubik's Cube. But, look, it doesn't take a hell of a lot of brainpower to be an effective leader: witness Ronald Reagan. Do you need street smarts? *Yup.* A good moral compass? *Definitely.* Knowledge of your own strengths and weaknesses? *Can't lead without that.* A high I.Q.? *Nope.* Too much brainpower might even get in the way of leadership effectiveness because really smart people tend to prefer doing things themselves.

What is needed is a high L.Q. (Leadership Quotient).

Here's a mini L.Q. test:

	Rarely					Always	
	1	2	3	4	5	6	7
1. Do you learn from your mistakes (that is, change your behavior when you fail)?	—	—	—	—	—	—	—
2. Do you listen carefully to ascertain what others need and value?	—	—	—	—	—	—	—

	Rarely					**Always**	
	1	2	3	4	5	6	7

3. Are you dissatisfied with your organization's status quo (the current level of performance)? — — — — — — —

4. Are you willing to put yourself on the line to make things better? — — — — — — —

5. Are you pleased to reward others (give them credit, celebrate them) when they make a contribution? — — — — — — —

6. Are you patient *and* persistent when pursuing a goal? — — — — — — —

7. Do you say and do the same things consistently? — — — — — — —

8. Are you comfortable delegating important tasks to others? — — — — — — —

9. Are you willing to be held accountable yourself for the behavior and performance of followers? — — — — — — —

10. Are you willing to share information? — — — — — — —

11. Do you enjoy teaching (coaching) others? — — — — — — —

12. Do you believe that you can make a difference? — — — — — — —

72+: High leadership potential (you've got the right stuff)

60–71: Adequate leadership potential (you'll need to do some hard work)

Below 60: Severe leadership deficiency (you're probably better suited for brain surgery or rocket science)

Iteration and Institutionalization

Oft told and true is the tale of Johnson & Johnson's admirable handling of the 1982 Tylenol crisis. After the tragic deaths of eight people who had consumed capsules spiked with cyanide by a psychopath, J&J recalled all Tylenol products from store shelves (at a cost of $100 million). Ignoring Wall Street's conventional wisdom that perdition is the inevitable fate of corporate "do-gooders," J&J accepted responsibility for the crisis even though they were innocent of any wrongdoing. Within a year, the skeptics had been confounded when Tylenol's customers had returned to the fold en masse.

The inspiring J&J case is often taught in B-School *ethics* courses. But, those who tell the story usually put the accent on the wrong "sy lable" (as my Hungarian grandpop used to say). It is actually a better *leadership* case. Six years prior to the Tylenol incident, J&J's then-president (and soon-to-be CEO), James Burke, had challenged his top management team to review the company's Credo, which had been written years earlier by its founder, General Robert Wood Johnson. The Credo had yellowed on company walls in quiet desuetude, and Burke thought that was hypocritical, at best. Because the Credo enumerated the company's purported responsibilities to its various constituencies—from customers to shareholders—Burke believed its leaders should (a) live by it, (b) take it down, or (c) revise it and then practice its precepts.

He thus assembled the company's thirty top executives and gave them two full days to come to agreement on one of the three alternatives. The debate that ensued was candid, thoughtful, and spirited (the videotape of the proceedings is an underground classic). The executives thoughtfully discussed what the Credo's generalities meant in practice and how they would have to behave if they agreed to live by its stated principles.

In the end, they agreed to make a commitment to the Credo (with a couple of minor revisions of language). Burke then asked each of the executives to go through the same process with their direct reports and then, in turn, to ask them to do the same, and so on down the line. But even that wasn't enough for Burke. He asked J&J's managers at every level to commit to discussing the implications of the Credo *once every year.*

It is probable that the outside world would never have known about J&J's ongoing, cascading Credo Challenge if it hadn't been for the Tylenol tragedy. While covering the company's response to the crisis for *60 Minutes,* an obviously impressed Mike Wallace asked Burke how it was that J&J executives seemed to know instinctively what the right thing was to do. Burke explained that they didn't have to resort to "crisis management" or "damage control" because, since 1975, they had been collectively exploring what it meant to practice the Credo's values—starting with its now-famous declaration: "We believe our first responsibility is to the doctors, nurses and patients, to mothers and others who use our products and services." If it weren't for the fact that thousands of J&J executives had been debating the implications of those words for half a dozen years, the Credo would have been, literally, no more than a "motherhood" statement. The ongoing discussions had made it operational.

In subsequent interviews, Burke explained why J&J's Credo was not the typical "mission statement" that hangs vacuously over the shoulders of employees in so many other corporations. Because it was a "living document," subject to continued scrutiny and reinterpretation (much like the Constitution), the Credo served as the glue that united each of J&J's 160 independent business units. Hence, it was more than an ethical reminder to employees. In Burke's eye, the iterative and cascading discussion of the company's purpose, principles, and values provided the self-reinforcing focus that allowed for nothing less than J&J's continued success as a business organization.

Indeed, in every aligned and adaptive organization, leadership is an iterative process that cascades down and out continually. It can start with a discussion of strategy, purpose, vision, or a Credo—whatever is appropriate for a given organization. In one company where I've consulted, the process began with a discussion between the CEO and her leadership team to clarify her roles and responsibilities— in effect, the team got her to agree to what they needed her to do. The team then committed to go through the same process every year with those who reported to them. Like Burke's team, they understood that leadership isn't something you pull out of a hat in a crisis; it is, instead, an institutionalized capability that must be re-created and continually renewed.

P.S.: When Burke retired, J&J's next CEO gave into pressures to discontinue the Credo Challenge because the process was too time-consuming and costly. Then, within a few years, J&J began to have both ethical problems and a marked loss of alignment among its business units. I have been told that the process has since been reinstated.

J

LEADERSHIP
A to Z

Joint Leadership

Many effective corporate leaders have two heads! That's because the challenges corporations face are becoming so complex that the full set of skills demanded of their leaders is seldom to be found in one person.

The two-leader trend started in the 1970s, when the risk-taking, entrepreneurial oilman Robert O. Anderson teamed up with the scholarly and eloquent Thornton Bradshaw to form a dynamic duo that would lead the Atlantic Richfield corporation through a decade of remarkable achievement. The years that followed witnessed the formation of many more joint leadership teams and "offices of the executive" in corporations around the world.

Although Anderson and Bradshaw made the coordination of two heads look easy, in fact, it is an unnatural act that takes great practice. Ford Motor's well-documented 1980s turnaround was led by two individuals: finance whiz Red Poling and "car guy" Donald Petersen. Significantly, their joint effort was nearly a failure. Poling and Petersen had been bitter rivals in pursuit of Ford's top rung. It wasn't until they agreed to acknowledge publicly the complementary contributions that they each brought to the party that a nascent change effort at Ford began to take hold.

Eventually, after much counseling and effort, Poling's and Petersen's public truce grew into genuine mutual respect for each other's skills. Only then did the silo-based conflict that had characterized Ford's culture finally recede. As one Ford executive put it, once they got over worrying about "Are we winning against each other?" they were able to focus effectively on "Are we winning against the Japanese?"

Part of the success of joint efforts is good chemistry—Disney's Michael Eisner and Frank Wells had it; Eisner and Michael Ovitz didn't. But overcoming ego is also a factor—Boeing's Phil Condit and McDonnell Douglas's Harry Stonecipher seem able to share the spotlight after the merger of their two companies.

In the 1990s, shared leadership became almost a necessity. The successful transformation of England's giant Asda supermarket chain was led by two individuals, both of whom admit they couldn't have accomplished the feat as a solo act. (See SHITMs.) The analytically bent, Harvard-educated Archie Norman provided the strategic framework and financial acumen needed to turn the company around. But to implement the change successfully, Norman found it necessary to share leadership with the more open and accessible Allen Leighton, who brought the required people—and sales—skills to the effort. Norman, who could easily have kept power all to himself (and failed in the process), was able to avoid that common leadership trap because he had the self-confidence to admit that two heads are often better than one.

As good as two-headed leadership can be, its usefulness is vitiated if the two are identical. The trick is to get complementary skills (for example, Bill Gates is cerebral, but his powerful No. 2, Steve Ballmer, is an implementer). As Bob Townsend explained before Gates was born, the best duos are like yin and yang: they say, "Neither of us is very good, but our weaknesses (and strengths) may be compensating." The trick is for them to trust each other and to "split up the chores, check in advance on strategic matters, and keep each other informed after the fact on the daily disasters."

Champion International's CEO Richard Olson takes joint leadership to the next step, *team leadership*. He explains why: "None of us is as smart as all of us."

Resources: *Robert Townsend, *Further Up the Organization* (New York: HarperCollins, 1988), p. 221.
*David Heenan and Warren Bennis, *Co-Leaders: The Power of Great Partnerships* (New York: John Wiley & Sons, 1999).

K

LEADERSHIP
A to Z

KISS

Among Tom Peters's many contributions to the collective understanding of managerial excellence, perhaps none is as important as his insistence on the virtue of simplicity. Tom himself can state in a pithy, memorable phrase what an academic writer will struggle unsuccessfully to convey in an entire tome. The 7-S framework of Peters and Waterman's classic *In Search of Excellence* neatly summarized nearly everything of importance found in volumes of convoluted management books. And Tom later showed how all great business leaders observe the KISS principle ("Keep It Simple, Stupid"). He taught us that Sam Walton, Herb Kelleher, and other effective leaders disciplined themselves to make things so simple that their followers would never be confused about what they should be doing and why. That Wal-Mart is dedicated to "low prices and good service" and that Southwest's employees should "make flying fun" are messages so simple that they cannot be further reduced.

But simplicity isn't as easy as it looks! (See **S**ound Bites.) Justice Oliver Wendell Holmes is reported to have said, "I wouldn't give a fig for the simplicity this side of complexity, but I would give my life for the simplicity on the other side of complexity." He meant that simplistic, ritualistic, and formulaic statements by leaders aren't worth rotten fruit on a tree, but the ability to present an unadorned idea that compels action is the greatest gift of leadership.

That's why leadership begins with the exercise of asking basic questions (*What business are we in? Who are our customers? What do we need to do in order to succeed?*) and ends with the truly never-ending task of communicating the answers to such questions in the simplest language possible.

Resources: *Tom Peters, *Thriving on Chaos* (New York: Knopf, 1989).
*Tom Peters and Nancy Austin, *A Passion for Excellence* (New York: Random House, 1985).

Knowing When to Leave

Franklin Roosevelt was (very nearly) the greatest president. He led the nation out of the Depression, knocked out the tyrannical Axis that threatened the world, and saved capitalism by softening the system's hard edges. But we also remember him at Yalta, in his fourth term, huddled under a blanket, too weak and tired to resist the lies and blandishments of "Uncle" Joe Stalin. Had FDR only quit at the top of his game!

There is just so much any individual can bring to an institution. George Washington could have had a third term, but he knew when it was time to leave (indeed, as much as anything, it was his refusal to hang on to power that ensured his high place in history). In business, CEOs like OxyPetroleum's Armand Hammer, AT&T's Robert Allen, Digital Equipment Corporation's Kenneth Olsen, and Estee Lauder's Leonard Lauder become so enamored by the perks and the power that they fail to notice when they've lost their touch. In many instances, the issue isn't recognizing the onset of fatigue or senility but, instead, knowing what you are good at (and, conversely, what your limitations are). For example, entrepreneur Nolan Buhnell has *started* some twenty companies. When he gets them going, he has the good grace and self-knowledge to get out of the way and let professional managers take the helm.

Silicon Valley's legendary Harry Saal, founder of Network General, is one of a rare breed of high-tech leaders with exquisite timing and grace. Having taken his company public, Saal, who was not quite fifty at the time, came to the conclusion that he had already made his greatest contribution to the firm he founded. Thus, he decided to pass on the exalted status of being a Silicon Valley CEO. Saal understood that the alternative to corporate power isn't death—as so many chief executives fear. Instead, he created a new life for himself as a mentor to the next generation of leaders in his company (and to those in other Silicon Valley firms as well). (See Tomorrow's Leaders?) He also became the "conscience of the Valley," plugging Bay Area schools into the digital age and chairing the Community Foundation of Santa Clara County. And, what's more, he's freed himself up to start yet another company!

LEADERSHIP
A to Z

Leaders
(Who's Who in the Twentieth Century)

Since the late 1980s, I've asked the same question of every group I've addressed: "Who comes to mind when you hear the words *leader* and *leadership?*" By now, I've benefited from the thinking of several thousand people on four continents, and I've discovered a remarkable consensus among men and women, scholars and business people, journalists and government officials from some forty different nations. Here are the names that are most often mentioned:

> Mohandas Gandhi
>
> Winston Churchill
>
> Abraham Lincoln
>
> Franklin Roosevelt
>
> Martin Luther King, Jr.
>
> Margaret Thatcher
>
> Theodore Roosevelt
>
> Nelson Mandela

Vaclav Havel

Jean Monnet

Almost as frequently cited as the last two names on the list are Golda Meir, General (not President) Dwight Eisenhower, Eleanor Roosevelt, Mustafa Kemal Atatürk, Charles de Gaulle, Mother Teresa, and the Ayatollah Khomeini. Several things stand out about this list:

- There is remarkable agreement among people from widely divergent backgrounds—and across cultures and natural boundaries—about who the greatest leaders have been. Although all the respondents may not have been able to articulate just what it was about these individuals that constituted their greatness as leaders, most people clearly recognize those characteristics when they see them (and the proof is that they see them in the same individuals).
- Mao, Hitler, Stalin, and other tyrants are seldom cited as great leaders. (See Lenin, Hitler, *et alia* to learn why not.)
- No business leader is among the top twenty most frequently cited leaders. Although Jack Welch, Bill Gates, and Percy Barnevik are in the top forty, for some reason even business executives seldom cite corporate CEOs as exemplary leaders (although I have noticed a pattern of managers publicly nominating their own CEOs!).

Lenin, Hitler, *et alia*

George Will was the first to offer a candidate for the "Man of the Century." In 1996, he nominated none other than Vladimir Ilyich Lenin. Not that Will likes Lenin, mind you; he just felt compelled to acknowledge the Soviet founder's remarkable influence, power, and overall skill as a leader.

Leadership skill? The source of Lenin's power, as he himself proudly boasted, was the barrel of a gun. Like Mao, Hitler, Stalin, Ho, Castro, and the other dictators, authoritarians, and "revolutionaries" whose names soil the pages of the history of this century, Lenin would have gotten nowhere without violence. Of course, like those other rogues, he was a silver-tongued orator with the manifest ability to manipulate the masses. He told them what they wanted to hear and kept his fingers crossed behind his back. But he didn't fool everyone. Those he didn't fool he shot before they could influence others by—dare we say it?—telling *the truth*.

James MacGregor Burns tells a story about a student who made the case to her classmates that Hitler was a true leader: "Bad as he was," she had said, "he mirrored the hopes and hates of the German people, he won elections, and he fulfilled his promises by changing Germany along the lines his followers wanted. How could he not be called a leader?" As Burns explains, the student's (and, we might add, George Will's) problem "was not confusion about Hitler, but about the true nature of leadership."

Yes, Hitler superficially addressed his followers basest *wants*. But he did not address their fundamental *needs*. To be a great nation, Germany didn't *need* to conquer Europe or exterminate the Jews, and Hitler never bothered to find out what the Germans really needed to restore their pride after World War I.

Yes, Hitler gave the masses what they *thought* they wanted. But he never offered them a full range of alternatives, nor did he show them the probable consequences of the one strategy he did offer.

Yes, Hitler won elections. But only at the beginning, and even then he was given to violence and coercion. And he never revealed his true agenda to the electorate.

Yes, he made good on some lower-level promises. But he failed to address fundamental social ends, the pursuit of which constitutes justice in all societies: Hitler was remarkably silent about such basic, universal values as liberty, equality, community, and economic security.

Yes, he changed German society. But not for the better in the long run. Not for the better, importantly, by the very measure that the German people ultimately used to evaluate their putative *Führer*: he led them to the total destruction of their nation. Clearly, if they had known where he was leading them, they would not have followed.

Hitler thus was not a true leader because his agenda was his own, his goals were his own, and the German nation and people were merely the means he used to pursue his personal agenda of power and megalomania. Burns concludes,

"He was a terrible mis-leader: personally cruel and vindictive, politically duplicitous and treacherous, ideologically vicious and annihilative in his aims. A leader of change? Yes, he left Germany a smoking devastated land. My student may have Hitler—I'll take Gandhi, Mandela, and King."

And what is the true nature of leadership? University of Richmond Professor Joanne Ciulla (another "student" of James MacGregor Burns) succinctly clarifies the difference between leadership and coercion: "Managers and generals can act like playground bullies and use their power and rank to force their will on people, but this is coercion, not leadership. Leadership is not a person or a position. It is a complex moral relationship between people, based on trust, obligation, commitment, emotion and a shared vision of the good."

George Will, are you listening?

Resources: George Will, "Man of the Century, Alas," *Newsweek,* September 16, 1996.
*Joanne B. Ciulla, ed., *Ethics, the Heart of Leadership,* foreword by James MacGregor Burns (New York: Praeger, 1998).

Listening

I've regularly led seminars on leadership in which participants read and discuss case studies, analyzing the actions of such statesmen as Gandhi, Churchill, Lincoln, and Jean Monnet, and such corporate CEOs as Percy Barnevik, Jack Welch, and Bob Galvin. As part of an end-of-the-course evaluation, I always ask, "What is the most important lesson you have drawn from your discussions of what great leaders do?" Eight times out of ten participants answer, "Listen."

At first I resisted this feedback. To my mind, the cases hadn't emphasized listening. I had expected the participants instead to cite such leadership actions as "inclusion," "respect for others," "creating disciples," or "acting with integrity." I figured I must have been teaching the cases in the wrong way, failing to stress the right stuff.

But no matter how I changed my approach—or even when I chose different cases—the feedback was consistent. I started to ask why, and what I learned was both logical and insightful: *the only way a leader can identify the true needs of followers is by carefully listening to their concerns.* That's why when people seriously study what great leaders do, the most important thing they typically pick up on is listening.

After a while, I got the message and started putting more emphasis on how leaders discover the true interests of their followers. *OK, OK, I get it. Now I'm listening* . . . (See **N**eeds of Followers.)

LEADERSHIP
A to Z

Management of Change
(vs. Strategic Leadership)

D oesn't it make sense that if everybody does the same thing, it must be right? Apparently, that's what Fortune 500 executives believe because nearly every one of those companies has attempted one form or another of organizational transformation since the late 1980s. Indeed, the imperative to change has been so powerful that it is difficult to cite a corporation that has not initiated a "change-management" process.

In this case, however, the common wisdom is belied by experience: something like 80 percent of change-management efforts fail to meet the expectations of the executives who initiate them. So why do corporations continue investing good money in what experience shows is a dry well?

The behavior of lemmings is a mystery; nonetheless, there are several reasonable explanations for the continuing attraction of change-management programs: They address the real and undeniable need for change; they make logical sense; most of the activities involved are necessary; and they are simple to understand and easy to implement.

So what's the rub? The fatal shortcoming of those programs lies, paradoxically, in that last virtue: their ease of implementation. Processes of change management may, in fact, be *too easy,* in that the responsibility for carrying them out can be readily delegated to the head of human resources or some other staff person down the line. That's probably why the leader of the organization is not fully engaged in the 80 percent of change-management efforts that fail.

If we review the most successful instances of organizational transformation, we find that none of them were delegated to H.R. types or any other designated "change agents." We discover that, in almost every instance, those efforts were spearheaded by the leader of the organization, whether it was James Houghton at Corning, Jack Welch at GE, Gordon Bethune at Continental, Percy Barnevik at ABB, John Browne at British Petroleum, Robert Galvin at Motorola, Lou Gerstner at IBM, or Harry Kamen at MetLife.

Of course, the actual work of change was fully delegated in all the instances mentioned above (and in many of the companies change-management processes were used as tools when and where appropriate). Significantly, in none of these successful transformations was the effort defined as *change management* or, apparently, even thought of in those terms.

As Robert Galvin explains, "We don't focus on change at Motorola, we focus on renewal." Galvin is also explicit in separating the tasks of management from the tasks of leadership. Indeed, all the efforts mentioned above were conceived as part of strategic change in the organization, and those who headed the efforts saw themselves as engaged in ongoing *strategic leadership* and not as heading a program or process of short duration. This difference is not a matter of semantics.

The two basic, and opposing, approaches to change—change management and strategic leadership—start from different premises. For example, at its core, change management is antithetical to leadership. Most of the people responsible for designing these processes are from the fields of organizational development, psychology, or other behavioral disciplines where there is a deep distrust of command-and-control leaders. That mistrust is based on years of experience that demonstrate the human and organizational costs that inevitably flow from Al Dunlap–like despotism.

As well merited as this concern is, it founders on the false assumption that the opposite of tyranny is the absence of leadership. That's why strategic leadership takes as given the need for an individual (or, in most cases, a group of individuals) to be responsible for defining a framework for change and holding people accountable for carrying it out. Thus, in contrast with change management, the issue in strategic leadership isn't getting rid of leaders, it is creating *appropriate* leadership.

The goal of change management is to bring about a single, planned change in an organization. In contrast, the goal of strategic leadership is to create adaptive, self-renewing organizations. Put another way, strategic leaders are concerned with institutionalizing change by creating conditions under which their organizations will continually and habitually respond to, and anticipate, external changes in technology, competition, and customer needs.

Because the alternative to a self-driven, self-renewing organization is a reactive, static company that lurches from crisis to crisis, institutionalizing change in this way makes practical sense. Nevertheless, most corporations persist in approaching change as a one-off project—failing to recognize that even if they momentarily get things right, the world will soon change. They fail to understand that even the best plans, systems, and products inevitably become outmoded—necessitating yet another round of crisis-oriented change management.

Change-management processes typically partake of the characteristics of cookbook recipes. They offer step-by-step guidelines and procedures, outlining in minute detail who does what, when, and how down the line. This is attractive because it gives the illusion of order and offers the reality of executive control. Thus, change management doesn't need to be feared because it doesn't run the risk of getting out of hand.

In fact, however, change can't be managed. By definition, the work of change is an unpredictable, messy endeavor that involves trial, error, learning, and invention. Hence, strategic leaders don't try to handcuff the initiative, innovation, and creativity of followers to a prearranged formula with a predictable and safe outcome. Instead, the strategic leadership of change is about creating the conditions under which others will carry out the exciting and innovative task of discovering new ways to deal with a constantly evolving environment. As Crown Fellow Jay Marshall (see Tomorrow's Leaders?) explains, "In change management, success is defined as completing change initiatives on time, on budget, and with full capture of intended benefits. In contrast, strategic leaders see themselves as successful when people change their behavior and do things differently in order to achieve important business objectives."

Change management is concerned with implementing a solution to solve a problem; hence, its focus is on "how to." In contrast, strategic leadership is concerned with creating the need and context for change; hence, its focus is on the "what" and the "why" of change. Strategic leaders provide a vision, establish values, recruit disciples, and communicate the need for change. They create the environment for change: they provide resources, remove obstacles, and energize, enable, and reward followers. Those leadership activities are absent from change management, thus making that approach simpler, easier, more delegable—and less likely to be effective.

Moreover, because change management is process-oriented, it is relatively content-free (that is, not sufficiently linked to company-specific business decisions); consequently, standard process templates can be applied conveniently and inexpensively to any organization without much customization and without the tribulations of risky invention. And because there is little need for substantive input from top management, the administration of change-management efforts can be handled by staff people relatively low in the organization.

In contrast, strategic leadership is action-oriented and focused on implementing a corporation-specific strategic agenda. Because such agendas differ, and because the actions needed in any company are not predictable at the start, there is an expensive and risky element of improvisation in strategic leadership. On top of that, it takes a significant investment of time, effort, and commitment on the part of the top management team—and that is probably reason enough why the change-management alternative remains so attractive, despite its abysmal track record!

Strategic leadership requires time, risk, and a willingness on the part of top managers not only to put their own reputations on the line but, perhaps, even to change their own behavior. And that may entail trusting others to do the right thing— an attitude that runs counter to the instincts of many executives. In light of that, change-management processes are understandably seen as a more seductive alternative. Change management promises an easy and painless fix in which titular leaders can continue to do what they have always done while the H.R. folks try to change "all those resisters." In contrast, strategic leadership is plain old hard work!

Resource: *Bill Ginnodo, "Leading Change: A Conversation with Motorola's Bob Galvin," *Quality Digest,* November 1997, pp. 31–34.

Metrics I
(Evaluating Individual Leadership)

How do you tell the difference between a good leader and a mediocre one? How can a board evaluate a CEO's performance as a leader? And if you are a leader, yourself, how do you know whether you are succeeding?

These are such tough questions that most people in organizations don't even try to answer them. They beg the issue of qualitatively measuring leadership performance and, instead, rely on a quantifiable proxy: if CEOs make their numbers, ipso facto they are considered successful leaders. Indeed, few corporate boards have members who are capable of understanding data about leadership that aren't financial.

Doubtless, a corporation's financial record is the most salient measure of CEO performance. But should it be the only measure? For instance, shouldn't boards also want to know whether their CEOs are (a) building the human and knowledge asset bases of their organizations, (b) transforming corporate cultures to position their companies for future success, (c) creating benchstrength by developing successors, and (d) doing all that is necessary to leave a rich legacy for the next generation?

Because measures of this year's profit don't reveal much about such important long-term considerations, sophisticated corporations also attempt to measure the quality of leadership—and not just the leadership of the CEO, but the quality of leadership down the line. And thoughtful executives want and need such metrics. How else are leaders to know how they're doing?

When ABB's CEO Goran Lindahl was working his way up the organization as head of one of the company's largest business areas, he and his boss, Percy Barnevik, agreed to evaluate Lindahl's leadership by the extent to which he created "a self-driven, self-renewing organization." Lindahl was convinced that the means to becoming a self-renewing organization was (surprise!) *leadership*. In his view, leaders are people who pay attention to the external environment—monitoring changes in technology, competition, regulation, and, especially, customer needs—so they can respond successfully to, and perhaps even anticipate, relevant trends. To Lindahl, leaders create the capacity for adaptability.

If everyone had that external focus, Lindahl could be fairly certain that the organization as a whole would be continually changing and renewing itself without the need for crisis management. He was thus able to identify his key task: he first had to change the company's navel-gazing engineers into managers, then change those managers into outward-looking leaders concerned with the company's big picture (and their role in it). Hence, the leadership metric he and Barnevik chose for his evaluation: *Lindahl would be considered successful to the extent that he was creating other leaders*.

Jan Carlzon, another well-known Swede, used a similar measure when he was CEO of SAS: he would know he was succeeding as a leader when he could take a month's vacation and no one in the company called him. He concluded that if the phone didn't ring, key decisions were being made without him, and, hence, others were leading.

Before Carlzon could measure up to his own standard, he had to change his thinking about his role in the company and then discipline himself to practice what he believed. The first time he came back from vacation, he discovered that some of the decisions that had been made in his absence were not to his liking. He was thus tempted to question, to second-guess, and to criticize those "wrong" decisions. Then he hit on an important insight: how did he know those decisions were wrong? After all, one can evaluate the quality of a decision only after the full consequences are known; therefore, all he really knew at the time was that the decisions were different from (that is, not objectively better or worse than) the ones he would have made.

Moreover, because the decisions had been made by people closer to the relevant action than he was, it dawned on him that, just perhaps, their decisions might even be *better* than those he would have made! Once Carlzon got comfortable with this profound insight, he was able to let go of his need to control. This had a positive, snowballing effect throughout SAS as people down the line became liberated to act as leaders. And when that happened, he had a true indicator of the quality of his own leadership.

When my friend Max DePree was CEO of Herman Miller, his leadership metric was quite similar to Lindahl's and Carlzon's. He concluded that, paradoxically, you can't tell anything about the quality of leaders by looking right at them. Max's measure was a bit like Heisenberg's Uncertainty Principle—that is, to evaluate a leader we must turn our attention slightly and observe the behavior of the followers: "The measure of leadership is not the quality of the head, but the tone of the body. The signs of outstanding leadership appear primarily among the followers. Are the followers reaching their potential? Are they learning? Serving? Do they achieve the required results? Do they change with grace? Manage conflict?"

Thus, there is considerable consensus that leadership is successful when followers behave as leaders. Nonetheless, there is a complicating factor: *time*. When can it be said with certainty that a leader has succeeded? As Charles Lindbergh discovered when he sang the praises of Hitler in the late 1930s (just before *der Führer* started to gobble up his peaceful neighbors), it is all too easy to make premature judgments. The safest course is to wait until leaders have stepped down before making the call. After all, leaders cannot be considered great unless they leave positive legacies, foremost and central of which are worthy successors. After ten years as CEO of ABB, Percy Barnevik stepped down at the ripe old age of fifty-five in favor of Goran Lindahl. Barnevik explained that if the company's success proved dependent on him, he hadn't succeeded. He left, in part, to demonstrate to the investing community (and to the people inside the company) that ABB had solid leadership down the line and not just one powerful leader. (See **K**nowing When to Leave.)

Sadly, it is this final test of leadership—succession planning—that tripped up Max DePree. Until that point, he had been like an Olympic steeplechase runner, gracefully clearing 2,900 meters of water jumps and barriers—doing everything right as leader of Herman Miller—when, with the finish line in sight, he hit the last hurdle. The two individuals who, in quick succession, succeeded Max as CEO both proved inadequate to the task. Indeed, because that last step frequently mars the overall assessment of otherwise brilliant leaders, Jack Welch, for one, is said to be spending most of his remaining time as GE's CEO engaged in the development of successors. Will Jack Welch be remembered as a great leader? We'll just have to wait and see . . .

Resources: *Jay Conger, David Finegold, Edward E. Lawler III, "CEO Appraisals: Holding Corporate Leadership Accountable," *Organizational Dynamics*, Summer 1998.
*Max DePree, *Leadership Is An Art* (New York: Doubleday, 1989).

Metrics I
(Assessing an Organization's Strategic Leadership Quotient)

It is necessary for organizations to evaluate the quality of individual leadership, but it is not sufficient. High-performing organizations are equally concerned with assessing their overall leadership capacity. Organizations that are full of leaders who have a shared sense of their company's mission, vision, and values—and of their role in making those a reality—possess a high Strategic Leadership Quotient. Companies with a high S.L.Q. achieve outstanding performance because everyone consistently behaves in ways that support organizational objectives and strategies—in short, everyone does the right thing and does things right.

Accurately and objectively measuring your organization's S.L.Q. obviously requires sensitive and appropriate techniques and tools. For example, telling differences often exist between the assessments of S.L.Q. made by individuals at different levels of an organization. With that important caveat in mind, here's a minidiagnostic that will help you informally rate your organization's S.L.Q. How does your company stack up? (Of course, the left side is the *wrong* place to be.)

What's Your S.L.Q?

	Rarely					Always	
	1	2	3	4	5	6	7

1. Can everyone in your company clearly explain the meaning of the corporate vision? — — — — — — —

2. Is there a clear understanding by all of what they have to do in order to realize the company's vision? — — — — — — —

3. Are conflicts resolved in a way that advances overall company goals? — — — — — — —

4. Do people on the front line routinely do the things necessary to achieve corporate goals and objectives? — — — — — — —

5. Is behavior at all levels consistent with stated aspirations? — — — — — — —

6. Are the best people in the company working on the most important priorities? — — — — — — —

7. Does every manager live the company's values? — — — — — — —

8. Does your top management team have the capabilities to execute the corporate strategy? — — — — — — —

9. Is the quality of leadership evaluated— and rewarded—at every level? — — — — — — —

10. Is there superior leadership at all levels of the organization? — — — — — — —

Resource: *Booz·Allen & Hamilton, *Do You Know Your S.L.Q.?* 1998.

Muddled Teams
(the Hewlett-Packard Way)

Hewlett-Packard has been one of the most innovative big U.S. companies for more than sixty years. It didn't get that way by accident. Shortly before he died in 1997, David Packard described H-P's strategic intent going back to 1937, the year he cofounded the company with William Hewlett: "We decided right from the beginning we would be an innovative firm and would direct all our efforts toward making important technical contributions to the advance of science, industry and human welfare."

The company has never wavered. It has organized itself for innovation—planned for it, measured it, rewarded it. Over five decades, Packard dedicated his leadership to creating the environment in which innovation would occur. He encouraged people to question assumptions, to reflect on experience, to take risks, and to experiment. He even had to deal with "insubordination" from persistent innovators.

Packard admitted that, on occasion, he and Hewlett made mistakes and failed to fund promising R&D projects. But this didn't discourage the most dedicated of H-P's engineers who, undaunted, bootlegged the rejected research ideas they believed in. The innovative culture Hewlett and Packard created was so strong that it, in effect, overwhelmed managerial "discipline." Did Packard then punish the insubordinate subordinates when he later discovered what they were up to? Nope. He just got red-faced, mumbled, and ate crow when their projects proved to be winners. (And what about the bootlegged projects that didn't pan out? Well, what he didn't know didn't hurt either him or the bottom line!)

H-P's third CEO, Lew Platt, leads in the same way. (See **G**etting Started.) He doesn't talk about managing his company. Instead, he says, "I spend a lot of my time talking about values rather than trying to figure out the business strategies." The most important value for him is still innovation. H-P still organizes for it: no more than fifteen hundred people are in a division; each division is self-managing; each division decides its own products; and there are no constraining edicts issued from on high.

Anarchy? No, says Platt: "The most important aspect of the management of this company is cultural control." His job is to remind people constantly what they are doing and why they are doing it. Then he lets them go to work. Admittedly, some managers at H-P crave more direction. But how can the CEO direct and control the creative technical work that characterizes almost all H-P's activities? Instead, what Platt does is create the environment in which people will solve problems innovatively at appropriate levels. Such leadership is contagious.

For example, one H-P division was taking twenty-six days to deliver a product. Not bad, but their competitors were doing much better (and starting to eat H-P's lunch). The head of the division was beside himself: *Why couldn't anybody fix the problem?* The reason: there was no single solution because the problem was incredibly complex, involving some seventy different computer systems and affecting the operations of dozens of different functions. The division head then approached the problem in the HP way: he appointed two managers to lead a task force.

The two women he chose were experienced, but they didn't have impressive titles. What they had was a philosophy that was a mirror reflection of founder Packard's leadership. They recruited an interdisciplinary, cross-functional, and multilevel team. They started out by clearly communicating the team's goal and underscoring that they had only nine months to achieve it. Then, they described the way in which their "muddled" team would operate: no structure, no hierarchy, no titles, no rules, and no plans (that is, no Gantt charts, flow charts, schedules). How the team would operate—what it would do and when—was up to *them*. There was only one condition: every day the team would meet to discuss and reflect on what they were learning.

So they started experimenting and, predictably, failing. Yet, never biting off more than they could chew, they found that the daily lessons eventually started to add up, the midcourse corrections started to work—and, lo, before nine months had elapsed, they were delivering in eight days, inventories were down by 20 percent, and service levels were up to boot.

H-P looks like it has magic: perhaps a crystal ball or a secret sauce? In reality, the teams are just good at experimentation, at testing new ideas and concepts, trying things quickly, then backing off if they don't work. The company learns from mistakes, and it doesn't punish those who make them. And it breaks projects down to manageable pieces so mistakes aren't too costly.

That's leadership the H-P way. It's no wonder its practices have been the benchmark for the world for more than a half century. Early in its history, it clearly created the capacity to make scores of small changes in order to keep nimble, flexible, and, above all, able to produce a steady stream of new products. In this regard, it has been a lot like the 3M Company, where all systems historically have been geared to encouraging small innovations down the line. Yet, in 1999, both these venerable corporations found themselves in difficult straits. Although they were masters of the art of small adaptations, neither seemed particularly adept at making a major strategic adaptation of the entire organization. Apparently, companies must be good at not only the "little a" adaptabilities, but "big a" Adaptability as well.

This is a leadership issue—evidence of which may be found above where Platt says he spends his "time talking about values rather than trying to figure out business strategies." Doubtless all great leaders spend, indeed must spend, countless hours communicating their organizations' values; otherwise they won't achieve the requisite behavioral alignment. But that's only half the trick. No matter how well aligned employee behavior may be with a company's strategy, if the strategy is wrong, the organization ultimately will fail. What we learn at HP, 3M—and other well-aligned companies that have created the capacity for continual adaptability—is that leaders also have responsibility for the overall direction of their enterprises. That's why true excellence is described as strategic leadership. (See Change . . . or Continuity?)

Resources: *David Packard, *The HP Way* (New York: HarperCollins, 1995).
*Stratford Sherman, "Secrets of HP's 'Muddled' Teams," *Fortune,* March 16, 1996.

LEADERSHIP
A to Z

Needs of Followers

"The ear of the leader must ring with the voices of the people," Woodrow Wilson once said. Leadership must begin with listening because there is no other way truly to ascertain the needs of followers. Yet, in practice, when people are asked what they *need,* they almost always reply with what they *want.* And because everybody wants something different—and wants are limitless—would-be leaders get into trouble when they try to respond to the literal wish list of followers. Simply put, no leader can provide followers with everything they say they want. That's why John Adams counseled that Congress "should not be palsied by the will of our constituents."

Paradoxically, both Wilson and Adams are correct, and it is in the words of another president, James Madison, that we find resolution of the apparent contradiction between the two sources of advice. Madison recognized that the expressed desires of the masses are mutually incompatible, self-serving, and seldom in the overall interest of the commonwealth. He thus concluded that although leaders must listen to the stated aspirations of followers, they should not become "prisoners to public opinion." Instead, leaders must "discern the true interests" of the public and ascertain the underlying needs they have in common but are unable to articulate on their own. Then, the leaders must "refine and enlarge the public views" and restate them in a way that transcends the surface noise of contradiction and self-interest. In this way, Madison writes, "it may well happen that the public voice [as restated by their leaders] will be more consonant to the public good than if pronounced by the people themselves."

Once having discovered the common underlying needs of followers, leaders then create a new, transcendent vision that not only is large enough to encompass the variety of needs but, more important, elevates petty personal desires to the nobler level of a common good. In so doing, leaders hold out the promise to all of a better end than the ones they had dreamed of individually. The clearest example of such public leadership is Lincoln's Gettysburg Address, in which he described to a people torn by factionalism what it was that they had in common as a nation and why it was in the self-interest of all to rededicate themselves to realizing the American prospect.

It is far easier in a corporate context than in statecraft for leaders to find the common denominator that unites followers, gives them hope, and inspires them to act as one. Whether that common need is pride, recognition, security, or satisfaction from a job well done, it is the task of the leader to ascertain it and then to articulate it in a way that is clearer than it is when followers attempt to do so. In sum, leadership begins with listening and ends with creating the conditions under which followers can realize their true needs and highest aspirations.

O

LEADERSHIP A to Z

Obsession

Most corporate executives view leadership as what they do when they aren't engaged in the "real work" of business. Even among CEOs who talk the leadership game, few, in fact, devote the requisite time to the things leaders must do, especially to listening and communicating. And it is the rare executive, indeed, who takes seriously the task of developing other leaders. When push comes to shove, most executives simply don't have time for leadership development.

An exception is Pepsico's Roger Enrico, who is as obsessive about leadership development as Sam Walton was obsessive about Wal-Mart's customer service or Bill Gore was obsessive about innovation at W. L. Gore (see Communication). In the two years before he became CEO, then-president Enrico spent fully one-third of his time developing the next generation of Pepsico's leaders. In week-long seminars conducted at his home, Enrico engaged nine executives per session in a process that included coaching and an "action learning" project. In those projects, executives designed their own learning experiences, agreeing to take on an important, and real, challenge facing Pepsico. Some months later, the teams regrouped with Enrico to debrief and reflect on what they learned from their experiences. Not only was Enrico's pedagogy consistent with the state of the art of leadership development (see Training); but, more important, his own role exemplified the highest-order functions of a leader: coach, teacher, and leader of leaders.

Enrico could have delegated the task of leadership development to H.R. and dropped into training sessions for cameo appearances, the way most CEOs and presidents do. But, for some activities, obsessive behavior not only is appropriate, it is the only way to get the job done right.

Of course, there is a downside to such obsessive behavior: if it is not appropriate—and effective—a leader runs the considerable risk of being viewed as slightly unbalanced! In Enrico's case, Pepsico's relatively poor performance since he has become CEO has caused critics to carp that his one-man training program was, in fact, an egotistical exercise: *what made him think he was qualified to teach a state-of-the-art leadership course?*

Instead, he might have followed the lead of the more humble—and effective—John Biggs, CEO of TIAA-CREF (the world's largest private pension fund). Biggs is every bit as obsessive as Enrico about the need for leadership development, perhaps more so. Over the course of two years, Biggs insisted that his company's hundred top executives all participate—twenty at a time—in a week-long leadership seminar. Biggs himself attended a prototype of the seminar, then commissioned a customized redesign to meet the specific challenges the giant financial corporation was about to face. Before each seminar, Biggs met with participants to underscore the purpose and importance of the event. Then, a few months after each seminar, he met with them again to review the results of the action learning projects they had initiated at the seminar.

Significantly, Biggs has the reputation of running the tightest ship in the financial industry—the company doesn't waste a dime on administrative overhead, let alone frills. Indeed, knowledgeable observers had been shocked to learn that the normally tight-fisted company had invested in the industry's most ambitious leadership-training effort. What was TIAA doing spending a bundle (at least for them) on an activity that everybody knows has no payoff? Then, two years later, Biggs showed them when he produced a windfall return on the investment. In the interim, potential misfortune had struck when the U.S. Congress rescinded a tax advantage that TIAA had historically enjoyed, the consequence of which was either (a) the company would turn turtle or (b) it would have to succeed in one of the nation's most innovative and competitive market places. It turned out that, in part because TIAA's executives had been preparing themselves to lead change, the company was able to quickly transform itself from a relatively bureaucratic monopoly into a competitive tiger without losing a beat! Thus, John Biggs had anticipated the challenge. Now that's the kind of (appropriate and effective) obsessive behavior leaders should emulate!

Resource: Noel Tichy (as told to Eli Cohen), *The Leadership Engine* (New York: HarperCollins, 1997).

P

LEADERSHIP
A to Z

Paradoxes

Several years back, political scientist Thomas Cronin wrote an influential paper (circulated widely by samizdat) on the paradoxical nature of leadership. He noted that Americans want forceful leadership but, at the same time, are suspicious of strong leaders. Although they want leaders to be bold, innovative, and "out front," paradoxically, they want leaders to take them only where they want to go.

Moreover, Cronin pointed out that the positive characteristics of leaders are, in fact, negatives when they are excessive (or when they stand alone without counterbalancing virtues). Thus, although courage is essential, leaders who are nothing but courageous are, in fact, foolhardy (Evel Knievel was all courage, but he was *not* a leader because no one was nuts enough to follow him). Vision is likewise a necessary component of leadership, but people who are all vision are ineffectual dreamers (perhaps that is why few professors are leaders). And although persistency, consistency, and resolve are requisite leadership traits, too much of those good things leads to self-defeating inflexibility and stubbornness. Margaret Thatcher presents an instructive case in point. Both her admirers and her critics agree that no leader ever spent more time walking the particularly fine line between creating followers (who saw her as principled) and generating enemies (who found her inflexible) than did Mrs. T.

Successful leaders are able to appreciate (and live with) the fact that their calling is replete with paradoxes of all manner and complexity. Leadership requires simultaneous Alignment and Adaptability (see Change: The Task of Leadership); leaders don't do much, yet they are indispensible (see Energy); and most change activities are delegated, yet successful transformations require strategic leadership (see Management of Change).

Indeed, all leadership is about resolving paradoxes and managing a series of necessary tensions in the absence of clear knowledge of where to draw the line. That fact, perhaps more than any other, explains why leadership is so often called an art. The practical consequences of managing tension are felt every day in business. Corporate leaders are continually faced with seemingly impossible choices between such considerations as long term vs. short term, people vs. profits, and continuity vs. change. It is obvious that the answer is seldom either/or. Instead, it is *both*—with a little more emphasis on one concern than the other. Where that emphasis is placed, and how, is the essence of the art of leadership. Leaders learn to draw the line effectively in the same way artists learn to draw sure and confident lines on a blank sheet: through practice and through reflection on experience.

Resource: *Thomas E. Cronin and Michael A. Genovese, *The Paradoxes of the American Presidency* (New York: Oxford University Press, 1998).

People*Soft?*

At the spanking-new "campus" of software giant PeopleSoft, every day is "dress-down" Friday. The company's motto is "It's mandatory that we have fun here." There is little hierarchy, there are no secretaries (even executives answer their own phones and type their own letters), and there is only one cardinal rule: "Treat fellow employees, customers, and the bagel delivery people, with the same respect and courtesy you'd offer Jerry Garcia." *Bagels and Jerry Garcia*? Not surprisingly, this company has its own official rock band—the Raving Daves—named after CEO Dave Duffield (who occasionally jams with the group). Because the average age of its employees is twenty something, it is premature for PeopleSoft to hold a Bring Your Daughter to Work Day (so they have a Take Your Parents to Work Day instead). When Duffield decided that the company's mission statement needed reworking, he sent an e-mail to all six thousand employees asking for their input. And he heeded their advice.

OK, you get the idea. For all its fun and games, PeopleSoft takes the task of creating a motivating corporate culture *very seriously*. Duffield believes that the only way the firm can catch the industry leader, Germany's SAP, is if every employee is as dedicated as he is to solving the software-systems problems of PeopleSoft's two thousand large corporate clients.

Duffield is a tough competitor. Moreover, he is a hard-driving, finance-oriented capitalist who is personally worth some $2 billion, and he ain't satisfied yet. At fifty-seven, he's old for the computer industry—old enough to have learned by virtue of experience that you can be a tough competitor without being hard on your people. As he has grown from being an engineer to being an entrepreneur and, finally, to being a leader, he has learned that you can ask a lot more of followers if you don't run a salt mine. Work camps, prisons—and conventional offices and factories—require phalanxes of guards, supervisors, and managers to keep people working. In contrast, there are no supervisors on college campuses because professors are *self*-motivated. What Duffield is about at PeopleSoft is creating a campuslike environment in which all his employees can behave like self-motivated professionals.

Make no mistake about it, what Duffield does runs counter to the assumptions managers often make about workers. For many managers, a workplace is more like a kindergarten than a university. Managers who believe that employees lack sufficient motivation, commitment, and self-discipline conclude they must hover over workers to keep them on task (fully expecting that all hell will break loose when they visit the restroom).

And that's just the half of it: deep down, many managers fear they are not up to the leadership positions they hold and that workers can see right through their veneer of authority. In essence, then, Duffield has successfully stared down the hobgoblin that has haunted insecure leaders since at least the time of the Pharaohs: *the fear of appearing weak.* In *Antigone,* Sophocles (495–406 B.C.) tells the story of Creon, king of Thebes, who refuses to listen to the pleas of his subjects when they ask him to grant mercy to his obdurately principled niece (the eponymous Antigone).

Sophocles then shows how the insecure Creon's fear-induced toughness causes his self-destruction.

For those who prefer cartoon versions of the classics, the same timeless theme is restated in the 1998 film *The Prince of Egypt,* in which Rameses II refuses Moses's pleas to "Let my people go." The Pharaoh doesn't want to look like a softie, so he gives a hardhearted refusal to Moses and, in the process, inflicts trouble on himself the likes of which you wouldn't believe! Ditto the modern corporate world, where insecure managers from Frank Lorenzo to Al Dunlap devote hours to public displays of toughness only to garner classically counterproductive results.

As an experiment in leadership, here's an exercise you might try at the salt mine (or kindergarten) where you work. Like Dave Duffield, run the risk of appearing soft: listen to the people who report to you, involve them in decision making, and treat them like adults who are capable of self-motivation. Then see for yourself whose people are the most productive: (a) the folks who report to your Pharaonic, whip-cracking colleagues, (b) those who report to the hovering scold à la P.S. 42, or (c) the followers of that old softie, you. Of course, you also have to challenge your people and hold them accountable. That's what "soft" leaders like Dave Duffield do.

Postscript: Like every other company in its fast-changing business, PeopleSoft found itself in troubled waters in 1999. Again, the issue was leadership. Duffield was having trouble shifting the strategic focus of his company to the more promising arena of e-commerce. Like other successful high-tech leaders who had mastered the arts of alignment and "little a" adaptability, Duffield seemed less sure of himself in the strategic realm of "big A" Adaptability. Perhaps, like H-P's Lew Platt, he simply lacked the energy at age fifty-eight to lead the company through another grueling round of change. Or, more fundamentally, he may provide yet another example of the chronic inability of Silicon Valley managers to master the art of strategic leadership (see Comparative Advantage).

Only time will tell the full tale at PeopleSoft. But while we wait, one thing is already clear: Duffield's initial instincts in dealing with the crisis were a classic lesson in how contingency leadership inevitably ruins the best-intentioned people. Duffield overreacted to the cries from Wall Street "to do something" and decided the way to show that he was a tough, take-charge leader was to lay off 430 people—even as the company was announcing a 15 percent profit gain on 40 percent sales growth. By suddenly and inconsistently abandoning his sheep's clothing for a wolf's frock, he severely damaged his credibility with his employees and put at risk the trust he had spent years creating. The mystery is why leaders so often respond to a crisis by abandoning the very values and principles that led to their success (see Trust)!

Perfection

I t's unattainable in this life. Because all human beings are flawed, there are no perfect leaders. Even five corporate CEOs who experts cite as "best of breed" occasionally manifest imperfections that have adversely affected their organizations. Percy Barnevik's relentless twelve-hours-a-day, seven-days-a-week, fifty-two-weeks-a-year pursuit of excellence needlessly burnt out many good managers during his tenure at ABB. Jack Welch's early days at GE were compromised when he verbally abused a number of executives, a failing compounded by his subsequent prideful refusal to own up to the fact that it is morally wrong for leaders to disrespect followers. Jan Carlzon kidded himself about his shortcomings as a strategist and was in deep denial when he thought he could change the behavior of SAS's alliance partner—and chronic "bad boy"—Frank Lorenzo. Max DePree botched the important task of developing an able successor at Herman Miller (perhaps he failed because succession planning was a too powerful reminder of his own mortality?). And Michael Eisner's overweening ego occasionally causes him to become involved unnecessarily in minutiae at Disney, to fail to see when he is making a mistake, and to strut about unbecomingly in public.

Of course, the above probably would not admit to those failings (that's the essence of human imperfection!). And given their tremendous strengths and mind-boggling track records, it could be seen as petty and churlish to mention them. Indeed, I wouldn't bother to make such a big deal out of such (relatively) minor flaws if the "myth of perfection" wasn't such a powerful source of confusion among would-be leaders.

So here are the lessons. Relax if you occasionally screw up 'cause nobody's perfect! And, more important, don't let the inevitable imperfections of potentially valuable role models get in the way of your learning from their experiences. It is self-defeating to say, "I can't use X as a model because X screwed the pooch by doing Y." Instead, learners will ask, "Despite X's shortcomings, what can I learn from all the great stuff she did as a leader?" So learn from your own mistakes, learn from the mistakes (and positive experiences) of others, and remember what Eric Hoffer said: "It is the learners who inherit the future."

Performance
(Hard-Edged)

Question: What would the editors of the *Wall Street Journal* call a leader who says his goal is to create a sense of community based on trust in which the highest principle is "respect for people"?

Answer: A wimp.

Many critics assume that leaders who care about their employees—and who actively encourage their participation and solicit their ideas—are softies who don't care about hard-edged business performance. They ought to meet Jack Stack.

Stack, the CEO of Springfield ReManufacturing, is renowned in small-business circles for having turned around a failing rust-belt company, multiplying the value of its stock by 18,300 percent in six years, and creating six hundred new jobs in the process. His secret? *He trusted his employees with real managerial information.* Stack practices "open-book management," in which every employee has access to all the numbers. Not only do they all see the company's income and cash-flow statements and balance sheet, they have all been taught how to read, interpret, and then apply the information found in such financial reports. Blue-collar workers, secretaries, everybody at SpringfieldRe is thus given the equivalent of a college business education.

In 1982, Stack and 119 workers and managers bought the company from International Harvester for $9 million ($8.9 million of which was borrowed). Immediately, Stack realized that they were in trouble. The reality of the situation was that they were faced with servicing an enormous debt and meeting a payroll—but without the advantages of capital, a solid customer base, advanced technology, or a sophisticated workforce. Stack decided that the place to start was with the workforce: "They're fantastic people," he says, "but no one had ever given them the tools to do the job right."

Stack reasoned that the most important of those tools is information—which is not at all an obvious conclusion in the old-line, grungy business of rebuilding engines for the used truck and tractor market. Still, he believed that if his people knew how their own performance translated into the company's overall ability to compete—and if they had the authority to act on that knowledge—workers would start to think like managers, and everyone would start to act as if they owned the business. In his book, *The Great Game of Business,* Stack explains how it all works in practice:

> Suppose we're paying $26 an hour for labor and overhead, and a guy decided to rework a connecting rod, which would cost us $45 new. If it takes him one hour, the company makes money. If it takes him two hours, we lose money. And it has to be his judgment call, because no two salvage jobs are exactly the same. So people constantly have to decide whether it pays to put in the time and effort required to do a particular operation.

Cost control happens (or doesn't happen) on the level of the individual. You don't become the least-cost producer by issuing edicts from an office, or by setting up elaborate systems and controls, or by giving pep talks. The best way to control costs is to enlist everyone in the effort. That means providing people with the tools that allow them to make the right decisions. Those tools are our magic numbers.

So it's management by the numbers at SpringfieldRe—rows and columns of hard-edged numbers that everybody generates daily and feeds to the finance department, where, in turn, they are aggregated and distributed as weekly reports to each department in the company. Then, everybody analyzes the data to see how they are doing and where they can do better. For example, a cam-rod rebuilder might decide to analyze the "overhead absorption" numbers for his department (the percentage of corporate overhead expenses covered by the department's productivity) and then find ways to reduce those costs. The net effect, according to the company's CFO, "is like having 700 internal auditors out there in every function of the company." Because everyone owns a share of the business and all participate in gain-sharing, each and all care about cost, waste, productivity, and profitability.

Stack's leadership philosophy is simple: "The best, most efficient, most profitable way to operate a business is to give everybody in the company a voice in saying how the company is run, and a stake in the financial outcome, good or bad." Cynical *Wall Street Journal* sorts—and, ironically, their Neanderthal cousins in the labor-union movement—might argue that such a philosophy is just old-fashioned manipulation, a modern offshoot of Frederick Winslow Taylor's piecework pay scheme. In fact, the approach is both ethical and efficient.

For participation to be both effective and legitimate, two things must occur. First, employees must participate in the decisions that affect their own work. Second, employees must participate in the financial gains that come as a result of their efforts. Participation in decision making alone is unethical because workers will see all the fruits of their efforts reaped by others. And participation in financial gains alone is ineffective because workers are powerless to influence the things that determine the size of their paychecks.

The genius of Stack's "great game of business" is that it combines the two necessary dimensions of participation. And both the human and the financial results at SpringfieldRe are impressive. As one woman blue-collar worker explains the "game": "To me, it means that I'm not just a name on a timecard. I'm a person, and what I have to say means something. I matter." And, of course, there's the bottom line: an employee whose stock was worth 10 cents a share in 1983 saw it grow to $18 a share by 1992.

Perhaps, after all, a leader can care about *both* people and profits? One thing's for sure, Jack Stack ain't no wimp.

Resources: *David Bollior, "The Story of Jack Stack," Business Enterprise Trust, 1993.
*Edward E. Lawler III, *The Ultimate Advantage* (San Francisco: Jossey-Bass, 1992).

Perks

In the memorable film *History of the World, Part I* (produced, directed, and written by Mel Brooks), the character King Louis XVI is catered to by hot and cold running servants. When the king (played by Mel Brooks) is out on a hunt and nature calls, an obliging servant (played by Mel Brooks) provides his majesty with a mobile urinal in the form of a bucket. The "piss boy" holds the bucket while Louis relieves himself, at the same time assuring the movie audience in an understated aside that "It's good to be the king."

Hey, wake up! One reason many leaders fail to live happily ever after is that they are in the game for the power (see **P**ower!) and the perks. Not only is it juvenile to assume that the prerogatives of leadership are limitless, but those who act out the fantasy always get their comeuppance. In fact, most would-be leaders who assume that they are accountable to no one never make it to the top, or if they do, like Louis XVI, they quickly are beheaded!

Gandhi understood that to lead is to serve. There is a scene in the film *Gandhi* in which he takes a tray from a servant and then he, the Mahatma, serves tea to the three men who later would become the first president of Pakistan, the president of India, and the prime minister of India. The lesson Gandhi teaches this powerful trio is that the task of leaders is to serve followers, not vice versa. In fact, he shows them that leaders will fail to attract followers if their goal is to use others to gain power and perks. Gandhi knew that the trappings of power corrupt. He thus gave up all his personal possessions in the selfless pursuit of helping followers achieve *their* aspirations.

I wouldn't advocate going as far as Gandhi (I'd especially advise against wearing a loin cloth in the executive suite). But, ask yourself, *Do you really need that corporate jet, the golf-club membership, the private dining room, the reserved parking space, the Herman Miller furniture in the two thousand-square-foot corner-office suite, and the Picasso over your desk*? Even if your board lets you get away with it, you will become corrupted by such perquisites and, worse, isolated from your followers. In particular, if you are a man, it's a fatal trap to claim the key to the executive harem. (And, it should go without saying, women are equally advised not to pursue leadership in order to fulfill adolescent fantasies.)

Even if you are a leader of a mid-sized organization or of only two or three people, do you really need the small trappings of office, the unnecessary class distinctions that too easily become the sources of envy? Get with it. The marines are right about this: *the troops (and the horses) eat first.*

Perspectives

Managers look in; leaders look out. An outward focus entails paying attention to the changing environment. *Good* leaders constantly monitor trends in technology, government regulation, and social values. They keep an eye on competitors, and, more important, they pay attention to the changing needs of customers. *Great* leaders try to anticipate change; they encourage followers *not* to use the best practices of others as a benchmark but, instead, to get out ahead and innovate so that others will use *their* practices as a benchmark.

Managers are concerned with today; leaders are concerned with tomorrow. A concern with tomorrow entails looking beyond this quarter and this year to where the company should be in the future. *Good* leaders think three to five years out. *Great* leaders paint a picture of what the organization should look like when the current management team retires—focusing everyone's efforts on creating a lasting, sustainable legacy.

At ABB, the goal is to discipline all the company's managers at all levels both to look outward and to focus on the future. For example, at the beginning of a management meeting, an ABB leader will ask his team, "What is going on in the operating environment?" He will list all the macro social, political, economic, technological, and competitive trends that his team is observing. Then, the leader will ask the team to list ABB's current strategies, policies, products, and so forth. Gradually, the members of the team will notice a disconnect between what they themselves see occurring in the environment and what they are currently doing.

In the midst of the embarrassed silence that ensues, the leader will ask, "Why do we do what we currently do?" The real answer, of course, is *because we've always done it that way.* But because that answer is self-incriminating, team members invariably will offer more defensible rationales: "what we do works" or "that's what customers want." At this point the leader needs only remind the followers of what they have said: "What works today won't in the future, and customers are starting to want something new." This exercise, called assumptions analysis, allows managers to see for themselves what they need to change in order to be successful in the future. It teaches them to think like leaders.

Creating an outward and forward perspective is as tricky as it is important. For example, in the 1980s, many corporations attempted to become more forward looking by engaging in forecasting and other forms of long-range planning. These otherwise admirable exercises overlooked the only thing known for certain about the future: it can't be predicted. Hence, today's most forward-looking leaders seek to build a strong organizational capacity for agility and adaptability. Instead of trying to predict the future, they create systems and rewards to facilitate and encourage vigilant scanning of the environment, rapid tests of new ideas, and the abandonment of past practices as they become outmoded. With this capacity in place, organizations can quickly identify external threats and opportunities for change and respond appropriately and with a minimum of resistance. The task of leaders is to create the conditions and systems under which this adaptive behavior will be institutionalized.

Resource: *Richard Mason and Ian Mitroff, *Challenging Strategic Assumptions* (Somerset, N.J.: Wiley-Interscience, 1981).

Power!

The power to command frequently causes failure to think.
—Barbara Tuchman

Power is the currency of organizational life. It's the real thing: the ability to influence others to accomplish something important and worthwhile. Hence, one wonders why so many wannabe leaders willingly accept a counterfeit of power: *command*. Command is an aphrodisiac. Otherwise savvy managers assume that because they are in a position to issue orders, they have real power. Sorry. In case you haven't heard, aphrodisiacs don't work. Not only are they ineffective, they backfire and lead to the loss of the very thing they were intended to obtain. The fact is, when positional leaders issue a command, one of two things can occur—and the consequences of both are the opposite of the exercise of authentic, productive power.

Scenario One: *The command is disobeyed.* Because commands are issued in order to be followed, a would-be leader doesn't have much choice but to punish disobedient subordinates. After all, leaders risk losing face if they fail to bring to heel those who challenge their fragile authority. Thus, in this scenario, leadership is reduced to a demonstration of strength. For leaders who view their role as akin to that of a cowboy who counts himself a success when he has broken a horse, such power displays are doubtless satisfying. Yet the ability to impose one's will on another—proving to the world "who the boss is"—has little to do with the leadership role of accomplishing a task. Worse, it creates a climate of fear and conflict in which whatever work does get accomplished is done begrudgingly.

Scenario Two: *The command is obeyed.* When labor unions really want to get the goat of tyrannical bosses, they employ a tactic called "working to rule." This peculiarly effective form of civil disobedience is used only when reasonable methods of negotiation have broken down. Then, workers simply resort to doing *exactly what they are told.* In fact, they *only* do what they have been explicitly ordered to do—which means they contribute no initiative, common sense, or off-the-cuff problem solving to their tasks. The result is work without motivation. When this occurs, productivity collapses, and angry bosses will demand to know, "What the hell is going on around here?" And workers have the perfect no-fault retort: "We're just doing what you told us to do!" Such passive-aggressive behavior is observable in many nonunion workplaces, as well, where employees will rebel (often unconsciously) against command-oriented bosses by withholding effort beyond minimum compliance with orders and rules. Paradoxically, then, obedience can be as unproductive as disobedience! (See Coolidge Syndrome.)

In all instances, hiring people merely to obey orders (or follow rules) is a gross underutilization of human resources. If work is that routine and mindless, it ought to be automated. The only reason to have people do a task is to take advantage of their ability to make rational adjustments, to improvise productively, and to use judgment in unpredictable circumstances. Who would want humans to act like dumb machines and respond by rote when the situation demands adaptive behavior? That's why leaders want followers to use their heads.

And that's why effective leaders aren't in the business of commanding or ordering and why they likewise pass up the ego-satisfying exercise of wielding brute force. Because leaders understand that their role is to achieve a goal through the efforts of other people, they see that real power—the kind that metaphorically "moves mountains" and accomplishes great business feats—derives from channeling the efforts of self-motivated followers toward a productive end.

For example, when Frances Hesselbein was president of the Girl Scouts of America, she had to motivate a volunteer workforce of thousands of people to start to do things differently in order for that organization to survive. Because her position had little inherent power to command, she realized she could not order the necessary changes in behavior. She understood, however, that by including as many people as possible in the process of change—by practicing "participatory leadership, sharing leadership" to the outermost fringes of the organization—the power of others could be harnessed to realize the important ends she sought to achieve. Her philosophy of leadership was clear and simple: "The more power you give away, the more you have." She shared a lot of power with a lot of people and, as a consequence, saved the Girl Scouts from extinction.

In sum, the question every leader must ask is this: "Why do I want power?" If the answer is "for its own sake," you should try to amass it and display it; however, if the answer is "to accomplish a task," then you should follow Hesselbein's advice and give it away! She had *real* power.

Resource: *Edward E. Lawler III, *From the Ground Up* (San Francisco: Jossey-Bass, 1996).

Purpose

There's a renowned graduate school for leaders, a place where the very best have gone to reflect on their experiences: it's called the University of Hard Knocks. Peter Thigpen is a proud alum of that venerable institution, and he has returned from time to time for continuing education.

He took his first degree at UHK in 1972. He was thirty-three then, and on the fast track at Levi Strauss. He had been appointed head of the company's European operations just as jeans became the rage all over the continent. Because the company could sell more pants than it could produce, Thigpen ordered a multifold increase in manufacturing capacity. Then, suddenly, Europeans took a fancy to bell-bottoms—and Thigpen was stuck with warehouses full of "unfashionable" (and thus unsalable) apparel. As a consequence, Levi took a $12 million dollar write down. The late Walter A. Haas Jr., Levi's CEO at the time, flew to Brussels with an experienced team who quickly put the house in order. Haas also demoted Thigpen. Pete felt he had it coming and even asked Haas why he didn't fire him. Haas replied, "Pete, we've invested a lot of money in your education. Now we want a return on all the tuition we've paid."

In the 1980s, this story was often told as an example of Walter Haas's greatness as a leader (which it was). But, during the next decade, the story became better with age because, in fact, Thigpen learned from the experience and gradually worked himself back up the corporate hierarchy. In 1984, Levi got that return when Pete was named president of Levi USA.

The story doesn't end there however. Thigpen continued to make mistakes, to reflect on those experiences, and to grow as a leader. He says that one of the things it took longest to understand is something that few corporate executives, in fact, ever learn: *the purpose of a business*. "I was taught at [Stanford] Business School that the manager's job revolved around P.A.T., cash flow, R.O.I., and quick ratios. After too many years, I learned that all of those measures are nothing other than a by-product of a customer who values the product you offer, who trusts you, and who keeps coming back to you."

Thigpen eventually came to understand why Peter Drucker says, "The only valid definition of business purpose is a satisfied customer." Indeed, because of business school miseducation and the myopia of Wall Street stock analysts, one of the hardest things for all corporate leaders to learn is that *corporations make products, but only the treasury makes money*.

Confusion about that fundamental fact is not confined to Stanford grads, MBAs in general, or executives in the contiguous forty-eight states. Britain's renowned guru Charles Handy finds that he constantly must remind his compatriots too: "Profits are a need, not a purpose." American, European, and Asian executives who fail to understand that basic lesson often take their eye off the ball, and, in turn, everyone down the line also loses sight of the fact that the basics of business are making and selling things in order to serve customers. Financial crises ensue.

Pete Thigpen became a great leader when he learned that the way to increase shareholder wealth is through serving customers and when he learned that his job was to focus the attention of followers on that singular purpose. (See **A**BCs of Business Success.)

Resources: *Charles Handy, *The Age of Unreason* (Cambridge, Mass.: Harvard Business School Press, 1989). *Charles Handy, *The Age of Paradox* (Cambridge, Mass.: Harvard Business Press, 1994).

Q

LEADERSHIP
A to Z

Questions
(Asking of)

Among the trendy pastimes in Hollywood is Michael Eisner watching. Like the informal trade in baseball cards, there's an underground market devoted to the exchange of Eisner anecdotes. My favorite (one I hope is not apocryphal) concerns the "option to buy" that the Disney corporation once purchased on Long Beach's Queen Mary (the dry-docked ocean liner) and Spruce Goose (Howard Hughes' stupendous wooden airplane). Disney executives contracted to manage those twin tourist attractions for a year, during which time they could test the feasibility of turning what, theretofore, had been a bottomless financial pit into a profitable theme park.

A Disney design team was charged with developing a "concept" for a park that would be so compelling that customers would gladly shell out 25 bucks each to visit it. The team agreed to report back to Eisner, plan in hand, within a matter of months.

Slightly ahead of schedule, the team members felt they had a knockout idea that they were eager to vet with their chief.

When they made their presentation to Eisner, he listened carefully and then respectfully asked the team question after question. As he did so, it was clear that Eisner had no preconceived notion of what the park should look like; instead, he put himself in the shoes of potential customers: What would they get for their money? How much time would they spend at the park? What would be unique about the experience? What souvenirs would they be willing to buy? Why would they be tempted to have lunch at the park? Would they bring the kids, make a return visit? On and on, Eisner grilled the team until, eventually, they decided that they weren't as far along in their thinking as they had assumed and that they had been carried away by their mutually reinforcing enthusiasm for their own brainchild.

The team went back to the drawing board, this time with a tighter deadline to report back. A month or so later, satisfied they had done all that was humanly possible, they returned to Socrates' lair. There, again, Eisner posed a series of tough, prodding questions, both speculative and factual. As he queried them, a consensus gradually began to build among the team members until, eventually, one of them said, "I think we've finally got the answer to our basic question: there's no way in hell anybody can make a silk purse out of this sow's ear!" Subsequently, Disney passed on the option to buy Long Beach's twin white elephants.

Let's analyze why this leadership situation has become the stuff of legend. During the entire process, Eisner never issued a command, barked an order, raised his voice in anger, or badgered/threatened/punished anyone. Personally, he didn't invent a strategy, formulate a plan, or even contribute a usable idea. In fact, he wasn't sure himself until the very end whether it made sense or not for Disney to build a theme park in Long Beach (or if he was, he had the sense to keep his convictions well hidden).

Yet it can be said that Eisner *led* the effort and led it brilliantly. Why? Because Eisner created the conditions under which his team could do its work effectively. And, at the end, he did what they couldn't do: he took personal responsibility for having invested millions of Disney dollars with nothing to show in return. Although Eisner might not have done very much, we can see, nonetheless, why this is cited as a sterling example of leadership in an industry where a leader is as rare as an interesting low-budget film.

As Harvard's Ronald Heifetz explains, "Leaders do not need to know all the answers. They do need to know the right questions." Heifetz has analyzed "the work of leadership" for many years and distilled the essence of what effective leaders do. He draws a useful distinction between, on the one hand, *technical* or *routine* organizational tasks that require administrative solutions or expert problem solving and, on the other hand, *adaptive* situations that require true leaders.

Adaptive leaders identify major organizational threats and opportunities and then frame apposite questions for followers to address. Indeed, in a complex world, most important issues facing organizations require the brand of adaptive leadership provided at Disney by the questioning Mr. Eisner.

In Heifetz's framework, the task of adaptive leaders is to get followers to face up to their responsibility to address real problems. Such leaders let followers feel the external pressure for change, maintain their followers' disciplined attention to the problem at hand, let disagreement among them emerge, and then "protect the voices of leadership from below." Leaders are thus "responsible for direction, protection, orientation, managing conflict, and shaping norms." But they delegate the work itself to followers because "it does no good to be swept up in the field of action."

Imagine what would have happened had Eisner pushed a pet theory— or backed one faction or another—in the debate at Disney. At worst, the corporation might have spent a bundle on the boss's harebrained scheme and, at a minimum, Eisner would have shut down a creative process of analysis. Heifetz concludes that, by standing back, leaders "are able to identify struggles over values and power, recognize patterns of work avoidance, and watch for other functional and dysfunctional reactions to change." By asking appropriate questions, leaders are able to replace sterile conflict with productive dialogue and, in so doing, effectively focus the energies of followers on productive ends.

Resources: *Ronald A. Heifetz and Donald L. Laurie, "The Work of Leadership," *Harvard Business Review,* January–February 1997.
*Ronald A. Heifetz, *Leadership Without Easy Answers* (Cambridge, Mass.: Belknap Press, 1994).

LEADERSHIP
A to Z

R&R

"When a man knows he is about to be hanged in a fortnight, it concentrates his mind wonderfully." Samuel Johnson's witty 1777 insight has become a "best practice" today, as leaders everywhere seek to create "burning platforms" in order to focus the attention of followers. Almost all leaders now know that there is less resistance to change in a time of crisis and, by extension, that crises legitimate asking their followers to bear pain. Moreover, because crisis seems to be the emerging order of the day, as Tom Peters points out, we must all learn to *thrive on chaos* continuously.

Still, leaders can't play the crisis card repeatedly. In real life, everyone knows that either the fire gets put out or the platform will burn down. Part of the problem is that people get tired of continually putting out fires. That's why leaders give followers a break from time to time; they let them rest and digest change. They even reward them with time off for a couple of weeks in Maui *without phone calls from the office.* (As USC Professor Tom Cummings explains, "Hawaii is better than Valium.")

Crises are draining experiences that turn energy into anxiety. And anxious followers aren't in the proper frame of mind to contemplate meaningful change or to build for the future. That's why AT&T's Robert Allen, Philip Morris's Michael Miles, and Nynex's William Ferguson are all *former* CEOs who lost their jobs shortly after setting their own platforms ablaze.

Smart leaders use the threat of crisis sparingly and briefly, and then turn anxiety into energy by creating hope. People who have something positive to look forward to—people who are building for a better future—have almost limitless resources of energy. What you have to remember is this: *anxiety breeds exhaustion; hope creates energy.* (See **H**ope.)

Reframing

Forget about the Duke of Wellington, forget about General U.S. Grant, even forget about Jack Welch. No matter what you've heard about such heroes, seldom is the success of leaders due solely to their brilliance as strategists. In particular, there are few examples of CEOs whose elegant strategies have lead to successful corporate breakouts or turnarounds. Instead, what effective leaders actually do is to reframe the way companies think about their existing businesses. Such reframings are often subtle; nonetheless, they can produce profound consequences for corporate performance—as demonstrated by Gordon Bethune's leadership efforts.

In 1994, when Bethune told his friends that he was thinking about becoming CEO of Continental Airlines, they told him he was nuts. The company hadn't made a dime in ten years; it had been in Chapter 11; its market capitalization of $230 million was less than the trade-in value of its jet fleet; and, thanks to the gross misleadership of its former CEO, Frank Lorenzo, the company was ranked last in its industry on every measure that mattered.

Bethune proceeded to confound his friends (and expert naysayers) by then leading the fastest, most remarkable corporate turnaround of the decade. It was accomplished by paying attention to fundamentals, including a little reframing of how the company's forty thousand employees thought about the company's objectives.

Bethune arrived on the job armed with several rather simple and commonsensical leadership notions: he believed the airline ought to (1) find out what its passengers want, (2) focus on providing what passengers want by measuring the airline's performance in those aspects of the business, and (3) reward employees for delivering the goods. It was a rather simple matter to discover what passengers were looking for: Continental polled its customers and discovered that number one on their wish list was on-time performance. Why? Because when a plane is on time, passengers make connections, they make scheduled meetings, and they get home as planned (instead of being put up overnight in a hotel at the airline's expense).

Obvious, you say? Well, it never occurred to Frank Lorenzo, who had assumed that the only viable strategy for the airline was cheap fares. To get cheap fares he had cut costs—jobs, salaries, in-flight peanuts, and passenger pillows all got Lorenzo's scalpel in a frenzied attempt to make money by saving it. Bethune explains, "We even had pilots turning down the air-conditioning and slowing down planes to save the cost of fuel." And the net of all those economizing activities? "They made passengers hot, mad, and late." So late that Continental had been stuck in last place for the previous ten years on the government's monthly ranking of on-time arrivals. So late, in fact, that Continental was losing customers in droves to Southwest, American, and United.

To refocus the airline from self-defeating cost cutting to the potentially effective objective of getting planes to take off and land on time, Bethune understood that the change had to be seen as in the self-interest of employees. In fact, it *was* as much in their self-interest as it was in the passengers': employees liked getting home on time too; and employees didn't like taking heat from ticked-off passengers who missed connections. Moreover, if the airline prospered, employees would have a measure of job security. All that should have been clear and obvious to employees.

But Bethune is a savvy leader who understands that what ought to be obvious often isn't. To really get the attention of employees, he knew that there would have to be a clear link between an objective measure of on-time performance and an unambiguous financial reward. He thus announced that each month Continental ranked among the top five airlines in on-time performance, each employee would get $65. How come $65? The company lost $6 million monthly by being late, so Bethune decided to share half the gain from improved performance with employees. The math was simple: divide $3 million by the number of employees, and it comes out to $65. To reinforce the point, he separated the bonus from their regular paychecks. The bonus checks were cut with the words "Thank you for helping us to be on time" printed on the bottom.

Here are the results of that little bit of reframing. At the end of the first month, Continental moved up from tenth to seventh place on the government's on-time ranking. The next month they were fourth (and employees got their first checks). The following month they hit first place—and have stayed there consistently. Over the next three years, the company twice was cited as the J.D. Powers "Airline of the Year"; its market capitalization grew to $3 billion; and, after having lost $204 million in 1994, Continental posted a gain of $556 million in 1996.

And what do Gordon Bethune and his executive team *do* as leaders? "We don't spend a lot of time on strategy; we spend more time on implementation, making sure we get it done. . . . The challenge is to keep people focused. We flew 2,200 flights yesterday. We've got to do that all over again today. There isn't ever a day we can kick back and quit."

Note that Bethune did not say his team spent *no* time on strategy. Again, the leadership challenge is to create balance. (See Muddled Teams.)

Resource: *Joel Kurtzman, "Paying Attention to What Really Counts," in *The Art of Taking Charge,* Heidrick and Struggles (January 1998).

Repetition, Repetition, Repetition . . .

Corning's Jamie Houghton gave the same speech, on average, almost every day for nearly a decade. In the process of repeating himself 'til he was blue in the face, he transformed a dying, old-line industrial concern into a competitive, modern, global corporation. (See Transforming Leadership.) His was a simple pitch about quality (basically Deming's Way, the philosophy espoused by the late management guru W. Edwards Deming), about values (integrity, performance, technological leadership, and respect for the individual), and about the responsibility of everyone to contribute to making the company competitive in world markets. There was nothing particularly original or sexy about Houghton's speech, nothing lots of other CEOs hadn't said. Except they said it once or twice, and they said a lot of other things too—sometimes contradictory, but most of the time just confusing followers about what *the* message, *the* focus, *the* basic purpose, and *the* goal of the organizations were.

But Jamie Houghton was a broken record (if you're under thirty, ask your mother). Predictably, reliably, relentlessly, and boringly, he spouted the same simple message over and over until everyone believed he meant it, and until everyone could repeat it verbatim in the event he was hoarse on any given day. Informants tell me that when employees saw Jamie striding down the corridor, they rolled their eyes and said, "Oh, oh, here he comes again!"

Why is repetition of The Message one of the most important things leaders do? Because people *forget*; because people get *distracted*; because people get so caught up in the intricacies of their work that they *lose sight of the purpose of what they are doing*.

Once, I was working at a company where the CEO had announced a new vision and strategy. He had e-mailed a copy to everyone, had sent them laminated versions for their walls, and had dutifully explained every word at a management confab. A few weeks later, he made the mistake of asking his top management team to go around the room and summarize the elements of the new vision and strategy that it was their job to execute. *Hem. Haw. Duh.* Talk about a deflating experience!

Try it yourself. At the next meeting of your direct reports, tell them to think seriously about something that you are planning to discuss at the next meeting. Then, next week, next month—it doesn't matter when—ask whether anyone can remember what the important idea was that you wanted them to consider. Don't be discouraged when one out of five remembers half of what you said.

People in positions of authority believe—because they have imposing titles—they can say something once (or twice) and safely assume that their people will have (a) heard, (b) understood, (c) believed the boss meant what she said, and then (d) committed themselves to act on it. Such would-be leaders don't understand human nature or the limits of their own power.

True leaders understand that it takes about twenty repetitions just to get from stage (a) to stage (b), and even then only their direct reports will have gotten the message. If they are to have half a prayer of changing the behavior of everyone down the line, they must devote 60 to 70 percent of the rest of their time in office to repeating the same message over and over. Being a leader is hard-slogging, repetitious work.

Resilience

Nixon, Reagan, and Clinton may not be names that are highly regarded among the fraternity of presidential historians, but you have to admit those three guys sure could take a punch! Like Mohammed Ali, time and again they absorbed their enemies' best shots and then got right back up on their feet (in Reagan's case, he literally took a bullet, only to bounce back to fight another day).

The course of leadership always contains far more down cycles than ups—even for those presidents who were greater leaders than the three characters cited above. Lincoln, Jefferson, Washington, Wilson, and both Roosevelts experienced deep and lengthy career setbacks that would have discouraged less-resilient folk. On the other side of the pond, Churchill suffered repeated failures and public assaults on his reputation—experiences made worse by his chronic, clinical depression—yet he managed to hang in the fray and never abandoned hope.

Such setbacks were relatively mild, of course, compared with those experienced by Elizabeth Cady Stanton and Susan B. Anthony, who struggled their entire lives through countless rebuffs and disappointments as leaders of the women's suffrage movement without ever experiencing the gratification of success. Likewise, Eleanor Roosevelt was subject to more negative criticism than any ten men could withstand with their egos intact, yet she never gave in to discouragement. (Yes, women *are* different from men as leaders: *they are more resilient.*)

Because of the inevitability of misfortune and discouragement, the ability to pull oneself out of the slough of despair seems to be an essential characteristic of leaders. Can the trait be acquired? Perhaps, but for those who take defeat hard, who get down on themselves when others get down on them, and who find it hard to "brush themselves off and start all over again," there must be an easier line of work.

Resources

Leaders have three basic challenges. One, they must establish and communicate the organization's vision, strategy, and objectives. Two, they must reward people for their efforts to realize the vision, strategy, and objectives. And, three, they must remove the obstacles that keep people from doing their work.

So it's as easy as one, two, three. If people know what needs to be done—and they are appropriately rewarded for doing it—then the only obstacle that will prevent them from performing effectively is the lack of resources. Here are the resources people need to do any job:

- *A System*. They need a structure in which to work, and they must be able to see the logic of their role in the larger process.
- *Information*. They need basic managerial data relating to costs, prices, and profitability. (See **P**erformance.)
- *Metrics*. They need to have ways to measure their performance.
- *Money*. They need a budget.

- *Tools*. They need machines and equipment (even if it's only a pencil).
- *Knowledge*. They may need training or education.
- *Authority*. They need to have adequate power to carry out their tasks.
- *People*. They may need a staff or help of some kind.

How does a leader know whether everyone in the organization has adequate and appropriate resources? *When objectives are being met, work is being done, and no one makes excuses when their performance is evaluated and rewards are handed out.*

S

LEADERSHIP
A to Z

Second Acts

"There are no second acts in American lives." At least, that was the view of F. Scott Fitzgerald. It is also the common wisdom about the careers of leaders. Indeed, it is fascinating how often leadership is portrayed as a one-act drama, the denouement of which is almost always tragic. Here are three examples frequently cited to support the contention that leadership is something that is done only once:

1. Winston Churchill, great as he was during World War II, nonetheless failed to provide the transformational leadership Britain needed to succeed economically and politically in the postwar era.
2. In the 1920s, Alfred Sloan transformed General Motors from also-ran status, well behind Ford, into clear dominance as the world's preeminent corporation; by the 1940s, however, the company had grown inflexible, sclerotic, and self-satisfied—and there was nothing that even the brilliant Mr. Sloan could do to stem GM's slide into bureaucracy.

3. Jan Carlzon led SAS's textbook-perfect transformation in the early 1980s, but when the operating environment changed less than a decade later, he wasn't able to repeat his earlier success—and SAS's fortunes collapsed in the era of global deregulation and strategic alliances.

Given such powerful anecdotal evidence, many observers conclude that transformational leadership is a once-in-a-lifetime activity. Indeed, the biographies of many leaders read like those of certain baseball stars whose careers are remembered by a single, dramatic, game-winning home run (and not by a high lifetime batting average). In this context, the task of change is portrayed as such an energy-draining endeavor that leaders are like—to shift metaphors abruptly—salmon who exhaust themselves in one heroic effort to swim upstream and spawn. The efforts of leaders to overcome the resistance to change is likened to the struggles of coho struggling mightily against the current and hurling themselves over rocky obstacles strewn in their path. If we buy this interpretation, leadership is a heroic, selfless, one-time effort in which courageous individuals sacrifice themselves to ensure the continued survival of their "species" (read: nation or organization). In short, you lead, and then you die!

Although this common interpretation makes for good theater, there are nonetheless more accurate—albeit prosaic—ways to think about leadership. First, and contrary to the common wisdom, there are leaders who hit more than one home run in their careers (or, if you prefer the fish metaphor, who spawned twice). Arguably, George Washington, Franklin Roosevelt, Charles de Gaulle, Dwight Eisenhower, and, in fact, Winston Churchill could be ranked among successful two-timers (and my own favorite government official, Elliot Richardson, successfully led no fewer than five of the largest U.S. federal agencies).

Second, and perhaps more significant, *there are countless leaders who transformed their nations (or organizations) in such a way as to build the capacity for continual renewal.* King Juan Carlos of Spain, Vaclav Havel of the Czech Republic, Mustafa Kemal Atatürk of Turkey, and Konrad Adenauer of Germany were each twentieth-century nation builders who created conditions under which subsequent leaders would have little need to engage in save-the-country efforts. And such corporate leaders as Motorola's Robert Galvin, GE's Jack Welch, and Intel's Andy Grove transformed their respective companies early in their long careers. After that, they could deal with challenges as commonplace occurrences—and not as crises that required repeated rounds of heroic management.

And, third, there are leaders who recognize that change is a never-ending task and, therefore, gracefully enable their successors to continue the ongoing process of adaptation and renewal. That's what David Packard did at H-P and what James Houghton did at the end of his career at Corning. (See **T**ransforming Leadership.) In the words of Walter Lippmann, "The final test of a leader is that he leaves behind him in other men the conviction and the will to carry on." It's true of women leaders too. (See **B**rownian Motivation.)

P.S. Apple's new, more mature Steve Jobs was the corporate world's comeback CEO of the year in 1998. By all accounts, Jobs successfully bucked the odds against a second act by reflecting on the mistakes he made the first time around and, this time, acting like an "adaptive leader." (See **Q**uestions.)

SHITMs

That's Store-Head Office Interactive Trading Meetings, of course! It's one of several imaginative techniques that Archie Norman and Allan Leighton used to breathe new life into England's nearly moribund Asda grocery chain.

When Norman took over as Asda's chief executive (just before Christmas in 1991), the giant corporation was burdened with $1.8 billion in debt, its stock had lost 70 percent of its value, and its market share was declining. Worse, a series of bad strategic decisions, coupled with antagonistic employee-management relations, made it difficult for anyone to see light at the end of the tunnel.

Enter Archie. He showed up at headquarters full of optimism, notwithstanding a December morn that was bleak even by the miserably low standards of English Midlands weather. Despite all evidence to the contrary, Norman was convinced that Asda's fortunes could be reversed. More surprising, when the company's top management assembled to meet Norman, he told them, "I am looking for your advice and disagreement." And, most amazing of all, instead of giving them a "put up or get out" speech, he *listened* for weeks before he talked.

Norman had recognized immediately that Asda's culture was dysfunctional. He soon discovered the causes: layers of entrenched, unproductive management, imperious barons who ruled over isolated departments (for example, buyers who refused to talk with store managers), and minimal, ineffective communications between headquarters and stores. Over the next six years, all this would be completely altered (along with Asda's strategy and nearly every other aspect of its business) by way of a continual process of change that Norman would co-lead with Allan Leighton (see Joint Leadership). Mind you, there was no overnight revolution at Asda, just an unrelenting, evolutionary process of adaptation that hasn't slowed down.

SHITMs was one of many processes Norman and Leighton used to foster effective communication and continuous improvement at Asda. Leighton freely admits that he borrowed the SHITMs idea from Wal-Mart (a mark of great leadership is the willingness to brazenly steal, and then imaginatively reframe, the best practices of others). Simply described, once a month Asda store managers were flown to headquarters where they were given license to confront the company's buyers, regional managers, and central staff with all the ways those high-placed folk made it hard for Asda's people in the trenches to serve customers.

The intent of SHITMs was to surface problems that management had been unaware of, to put real issues on the table, and, in general, to create a climate of openness and transparency. Moreover, Norman and Leighton had the wild and crazy idea that work ought to be fun, even the dead serious business of SHITMs. As Leighton explained to James Weber of the Harvard Business School: "To make it entertaining, we had this thing called the plank on this big table and it was like walking the plank. I asked the traders who they wanted on the plank, and they would pick a regional manager. The regional manager would get on the plank and the traders would attack him, and every time he didn't have an answer he would go further out on the plank.

It became one of the [company's] totems, and you would even hear managers outside the meeting saying we needed to get someone on the plank."

By surfacing sensitive issues in a safe and humorous context, Leighton reduced counterproductive backbiting and channeled energy toward effective problem solving. In addition to SHITMs, Norman and Leighton introduced such other intriguingly named meetings as "Saunas," "PAGs," and "PIGs" (Process Improvement Groups, to encourage quick experiments and share best practices across the company's two hundred stores), all of which were designed to keep up the level of enthusiasm for change and to ensure that it would never again be "business as usual" at Asda.

Five years after Norman arrived at Asda, sales were up by over a third, the stock price had quadrupled, debt was manageable and, for forty-four straight months, the company had been the U.K.'s fastest-growing retailer. In 1997, Norman decided to cut back his involvement at Asda to one day a week in order to focus his energies on a *real* leadership challenge: turning around Britain's Conservative Party. After the Tories took an embarrassing drubbing at the polls in the 1997 election, Norman assumed leadership of the effort to create a "New Conservative Party," one that would be as attractive to voters as Asda is to customers and for the same reasons: "We want a party which is more including, listening, and participative. But we also want a party which is cohesive, fast-moving, and able to engage in mature debate."

As this book went to press, Asda became a takeover target of several larger retail chains. Can its unique culture survive integration with a larger firm? Can its culture positively "infect" and transform the culture of an acquiring company? Sadly, if history is a guide, Asda's special characteristics are likely to be dissolved in the digestive maw of its predators. (See **G**randstanding.)

Resource: *James Weber, "Asda," Case Study, Parts A through C, Harvard Business School, 1997.

Sound Bites

The late Roberto Goizueta, Coca-Cola's renowned leader in the 1980s and 1990s, was a thoughtful, mild-mannered CEO who possessed incredible powers of suasion and motivation. He even managed to change the behavior of Coke's notoriously independent bottlers—folks who owned their own businesses and didn't feel beholden to the company's Atlanta headquarters. English may have been Goizueta's third language, but the man had a way with his acquired tongue. He could capture the essence of a complex idea and communicate it in a simple, clear phrase. One of his most-quoted lines described Coke's "infinite" growth potential: *each of the six billion people on this planet drinks, on average, sixty-four ounces of fluids daily, of which only two ounces are Coca-Cola.*

The first time they heard that line, Coke's bottlers and employees were knocked out by the originality, the clarity, and the audacity of the idea—imagine their closing that gap and capturing the sixty-two-ounce upside potential! And the tenth, twentieth, and nth times they subsequently heard it, the concept retained its power to motivate them to go out and sell the world another Coke.

Note that I didn't quote Goizueta directly; he said something close to the above so often, in so many different places, and in so many different contexts, that his original words are lost in time. And that's the point: it was never an ad-lib, off-the-cuff remark. It was a well-planned, well-refined, well-rehearsed, consciously chosen, and carefully communicated idea. It was, in fact, like many other pithy comments that Goizueta sprinkled judiciously into his speeches in order to capture the purpose and mission of the company and to motivate its numerous constituencies. In what is typical of great leaders, he had worked doggone hard to sound spontaneous.

On returning to India in 1915 to begin his long campaign for that country's independence, Mohandas Gandhi spent some two years refining his message before going out on the stump. He worked to make his appeal to the Indian people so simple, clear, and unambiguous that he could get it across even to illiterate peasants, in one shot, outdoors, in the midst of a milling crowd, and without aid of a mike.

Similarly, all leaders must spend hours identifying, refining, practicing, and internalizing the key messages they seek to convey to customers, employees, investors, dealers, and suppliers. Hollywood producers have it right: if you can't get your message across in a couple of compelling sentences, either you don't have a marketable story line or you haven't discovered it yet. Because it takes time and effort to learn what it is that one really thinks, more than one leader has had to go back to the drawing board for remedial work.

When leaders' messages finally become part of them—when they don't come out sounding memorized or rote—they then can speak authoritatively and convincingly on any occasion without notes and even without the need for inspiration (which cannot be summoned reliably). Moreover, when everyone on a leadership *team* has internalized an organization's key messages, they all can speak without fear of contradicting what their fellows are saying. That's why in the best-led organizations entire executive teams work together to hone their collective message.

Presidential historian Keith Berwick is currently the director of the Aspen Institute's Crown Fellowships—a prestigious leadership-development program for high-potential men and women in business, government, and nonprofits. Berwick, a four-time Emmy winner for his high-brow 1980s talk show, has spent much of his career practicing and teaching the art of communication. In one of his most grueling exercises—appropriately called Berwick's Boiler Room—he puts leaders through timed drills in which they must communicate their key messages under various adverse situations that Berwick throws their way. Berwick gradually turns up the heat until his charges can smoothly and confidently relate it all in under a minute. (*Impossible,* you say? Recall that a real pro like Goizueta could turn the trick in twenty seconds.)

Then Berwick challenges leaders to go a step further and "ask for the order." He teaches them that it is not sufficient simply to articulate their organization's mission, that they also must be able to explain clearly to their followers what is being asked of *them* in order to fulfill it. The first time Berwick's students attempt to "ask for the order," they typically mumble and fumble as the clock ticks away without their ever getting out a coherent statement. But practice makes perfect (or, at least, it leads to more effective performance).

Although even a two-minute message is too long in this age of thirty-second sound bites, in fact it has always taken a long time to prepare a short speech. In a more leisurely paced era, Winston Churchill—the undisputed champion of studied spontaneity—would devote hours to rehearsing and refining the bon mots that seemed to drop effortlessly from his lips. John Gardner tells the story of Churchill in his habitual bath (where the old bulldog loved to wallow by the hour, with brandy and a cigar, polishing his priceless words): "One day his valet, having drawn his master's bath shortly before, heard Churchill's voice booming out from the bathroom. The valet stuck his head in to find out if anything was needed. Churchill, immersed in the bathtub, said, 'I was not speaking to you, Norman, I was addressing the House of Commons.'"

Resource: *John Gardner, *On Leadership* (New York: Free Press, 1990).

Symbolism

I always thought symbols were those things musicians bang together.
—Marilyn Monroe

Leaders use symbolic acts to communicate meaning and purpose and to unite followers around common values. In 1920, Gandhi asked his followers to burn their clothes that were made of store-bought cotton and, instead, to wear homespun. He did so because cloth was a universal symbol (both Hindus and Moslems wore clothing), it represented dependence on Britain (Indian cotton was sent to Manchester, made into cloth, and then shipped back to India—with the value added staying in England), and its burning symbolized both the empowerment of the Indian masses and Gandhi's efficacy as a leader (Britain went into a severe economic recession when its textile mills were forced to close). To constantly reinforce Gandhi's message, the spinning wheel became the symbol of the Congress Party, and, thus, every time an Indian spun cloth for the next twenty-five years she or he demonstrated solidarity with the cause of independence.

No less dramatically, Merck's now-retired CEO Roy Vagelos committed that giant pharmaceutical company to giving away a drug that prevents river blindness, a disease that afflicts a million people worldwide, leaving over 300,000 blind in the poorest regions of the poorest nations. The product cost Merck $200 million to develop and millions more annually to distribute free of charge to those who need it. Many shareholders, Wall Street analysts, and some Merck board members objected to this "giveaway." They asked, "Is Merck a charitable organization?" Vagelos resisted those pressures throughout his long and successful tenure. He saw that the donations symbolized the values on which the company's founder, George Merck, had built the company: "We never forget that medicine is for the people. It is not for the profits. The profits follow."

And how could Merck's people forget the company's values when the river-blindness program constantly reinforced the higher-order purpose of their corporate mission? Vagelos understood that ending the program would have had a negative impact on Merck's culture; equally important, the pride Merck's people took in being associated with such generosity led to greater loyalty and commitment to overall corporate goals. In fact, Merck's profits were never higher than on Vagelos's watch, when strategic decisions were predicated on their consistency with company values.

Although Marilyn Monroe is the most quotable, she was not the first person to comment on how tricky the symbolism business can be. Of all the traits of leadership, the effective use of symbols may be the most difficult to master. (See **G**randstanding.) Yet when leaders do such relatively little things as sharing information, punishing those who transgress company ethical standards, admitting (and apologizing for) their mistakes, and even playing softball with the troops at the company picnic, they send messages that are louder and clearer than cymbals banging!

LEADERSHIP
A to Z

Teaching

In the popular press, leaders commonly are referred to as czars, commanders, chieftains, generals, masters, captains, bosses, superiors, and assorted other nouns that conjure up metaphors of power and command (and, by extension, the subordination of underlings). There is more to this choice of words than journalists consulting thesauruses for sprightly synonyms. In fact, the cultural equation of leadership with the rule of a powerful individual is rooted in thousands of years of human history and experience, going back to our club-wielding ancestors.

Nonetheless, for the last twenty-five hundred years philosophers, historians, and theologians have employed a different set of metaphors to describe a less-tyrannical brand of leadership. To Plato, Aristotle, Confucius, Mohammed, and the authors of the Christian Gospels, the language of leadership has been that of caring teachers, ministers, and mentors. In the nineteenth century, British parliamentarian and philosopher John Stuart Mill applied this teaching perspective on leadership to the world of democratic governance. He described elective office as "a rostra [the lecterns used by ministers and teachers] for instructing and impelling the public mind."

A few years later, Teddy Roosevelt applied the metaphor to the U.S. presidency, arguing that the real power inherent in that office was not the ability to command or control but, instead, the "bully pulpit" of persuasion and moral instruction. Later, his cousin Franklin would further refine the teacher's art in his famous "fireside chats."

In the twentieth-century corporate world, the leadership activities of GM's Alfred Sloan and his inaptly named colleague "Boss" Kettering, IBM's Watsons (Sr. and Jr.), Motorola's Galvins (Paul and Robert), the W. L. Gores (*père et fils*), and three generations of Haases at Levi Strauss all should be described using the language of teaching rather than the language of war making. And such contemporary corporate leaders as Intel's Andy Grove, Federal Express's Fred Smith, Boeing's Alan Mulally, and AmexCo's Ken Chenault similarly have earned reputations for being great teachers.

So what do teachers do that makes them effective leaders? They spend their time explaining their philosophies, explicating their values, and helping their students/followers understand how what they do contributes to larger organizational systems and objectives. Great teachers educe what is best from their students— inspiring them to perform at the highest levels by showing them what they are capable of achieving with focused and disciplined effort. Great teachers expand our horizons. And, especially, great teachers prepare the next generation to assume the responsibilities of leadership. (See **B**rownian Motivation.)

Team
(Selection of the)

Leadership isn't a solo act. That should be encouraging news to those would-be leaders who are *not* all-knowing, omnipotent, multitalented, and flawless. (Come on, 'fess up, you know who you are!) In essence, less-than-perfect leaders nonetheless have a running chance at success because they can compensate for their weaknesses, shortcomings, and areas of relative inexperience by surrounding themselves with people who possess the skills, talents, abilities, and interests they lack. That was the secret of the successful presidencies of Washington, FDR, Truman, and JFK. Those chief executives succeeded not, as some would have it, because of their personal brilliance but, instead, because of the talents of the brilliant people whom they attracted to work in their administrations.

Recall that Washington's cabinet included Adams, Hamilton, and Jefferson. Given that brain trust, it didn't matter much that ol' G. W. wasn't a genius himself. What he brought to the table in great abundance was an impressive level of self-confidence, which allowed him to be comfortable leading individuals who were brighter, more articulate, and, arguably, even more capable as leaders. In the long run, of course, his team made Washington himself look great—far more successful, in fact, than he would have been had he appointed nonthreatening nonentities to his cabinet. In the end, his team helped him secure a niche on Mt. Rushmore!

FDR, Harry Truman, and JFK all shared G. W.'s self-confidence. Moreover, when they recruited their leadership teams—their personal staffs, their cabinets, and other high-level appointees—they weren't looking for sycophants, cronies, or doppelgängers. Instead, they wanted people who thought for themselves, and they wanted people who would bring the highest level of skill, knowledge, and experience to the White House. Those presidents understood that their personal success depended more on the overall leadership capacity of their administrations than on their own individual talents as communicators, campaigners, politicians, or whatever their own particular leadership fortes may have been.

Yet most U.S. presidents have been far too insecure—or, perhaps, too egotistical—to build such teams of powerful individuals. And that shortcoming is even more common in less-exalted leadership roles. Most leaders in business, government, and nonprofit organizations are, in fact, *self-limiting* in that they surround themselves with people who are clearly no more than underlings. In this way, they dumb down their organizations as people at each subsequent level, in turn, follow suit and hire people who are weaker than themselves.

Threatened CEOs fear that exceptionally able individuals will steal their thunder. And they worry that, perhaps, when their boards catch on to where the real talent lies, a decision will follow to replace pyrite with actual gold. In fact, it doesn't work that way. Everyone respects leaders who are self-confident, who build impressive teams, and who give their people credit for doing what they themselves may be incapable of accomplishing on their own. Motorola's Bob Galvin, Microsoft's Bill Gates, ABB's Percy Barnevik, and Herman Miller's Max DePree are examples of very good corporate CEOs who made themselves into great leaders by drawing heavily on the strengths of others.

Theories of Leadership
(Top Ten List)

10. *Biology Is Destiny.* "The leader is the 'alpha male' with the most testosterone." Because humans are animals, deep down in our genetic hardwiring we—males, in particular—are driven by beastlike instincts to compete for the right to dominate others, or so say biosociologists (and the current CEO of the Progressive Insurance corporation!).

9. *It's All About Power.* "Might makes right." The Greek historian Thucydides argued that whoever is the strongest has the right to set the rules. (Contemporary version: "Power, and the right to rule, derive from one's position atop the organizational hierarchy.")

8. *Paternalism.* "The leader should be the brightest and most virtuous." Plato argued that the ability to lead was possessed by one person (or, at most, a few individuals) who, by virtue of unique skills and selflessness, deserves to be the unquestioned guardian of the benighted masses. (Alternative version: "Leaders are shepherds who know what is best for their sheeplike flocks.")

7. *Contingency*. "It all depends on the situation" is the advice Machiavelli gave to princes who wanted to know what to do to obtain and maintain power. Big Mac advocated the amoral manipulation of followers, urging leaders to exercise their "astuteness to confuse men's brains." Contingency theory—the belief that leaders should do different things and use different styles and approaches depending on what will most effectively allow them to achieve their own ends—remains popular five hundred years after it was promulgated. Also called pragmatism, realism, and Realpolitik, its best-known contemporary advocate is Henry Kissinger.

6. *Charisma*. "Leadership is embedded in the personalities of Great Men." Thomas Carlyle, the nineteenth-century Scottish historian, studied heroes who looked good on white horses (Napoleon, for instance) and concluded that they led by virtue of strong inner convictions about their God-given mission. Followers readily succumb to this "charismatic gift of spiritual inspiration," according to sociologist Max Weber (whose theory was later used to explain Hitler's, Stalin's, and Mao's uncanny power over the masses).

5. *Historical Determinism*. "The times create the leader." Tolstoy pooh-poohed the Great Man theory, arguing that even heroes are prisoners of historical forces beyond their control. Why was the newly born United States blessed with a surfeit of leaders—not just Washington, but Jefferson, Hamilton, Adams, Madison, and Franklin to boot? Abigail Adams had her theory: "These are the hard times in which a genius would wish to live. Great necessities call forth great leaders."

4. *Transaction-Based*. "Followers act in their own self-interest." We will follow leaders only when they help us get where we want to go, say some modern behavioral scientists. As an example, they cite Lyndon Johnson's transactional leadership when he was in the Senate: he constantly engaged in deal making—swapping goods, money, votes, praise, or whatever was needed in order to create followers.

3. *Reason-Based*. "Leaders lead by ideas." Followers of Christ were drawn to him by the truth of his teachings; Marx's followers were convinced that communism was right; and we choose our presidents based on who offers the best program and platform. This idealistic theory has few vocal advocates in our cynical era.

2. *Consensus-Based*. "Leaders encourage followers to buy in to a common program." Traditionally, Japanese business leaders were not commanders or rulers; instead, they allowed their followers to study and discuss an issue for as long as it took for a consensus to emerge.

1. *Values-Based*. "Leaders are moral agents and enablers of followers." James MacGregor Burns argues that leaders create the conditions under which followers can realize their true needs, aspirations, and values. Harvard's Ronald Heifetz builds on this enabling theme, showing that leaders mobilize and help people to solve their own problems.

Which theory is right? Here's something to keep in mind when evaluating them: theories 1–5 are about leaders who help followers achieve their needs; theories 6–10 are about leaders who self-centeredly get followers to serve *them*.

Tomorrow's Leaders?

I n 1997, the Crown Fellowship Program (see **S**ound Bites) was formed with the intent of identifying young executives who have manifested leadership potential. Such well-credentialed talent scouts as General Colin Powell, Levi Strauss's Robert Haas, Motorola's Robert Galvin, the Ford Foundation's Franklin Thomas, Network General's Harry Saal, and the Field Museum's John McCarter engage in an annual process of identifying—and then mentoring—an elite group of young men and women who show great promise to become enlightened leaders of both their organizations and their communities. Here are a few names from among the first two classes of Crown Fellows:

- Donna Auguste, CEO, Freshwater Software
- Aneel Bhusri, senior vice president, PeopleSoft, Inc.
- Deborah Coleman, CEO, Merix Corporation
- Lounette Dyes, cofounder, Cogit Corporation
- Christina Jones, president, pcOrder.com, Inc.

- Steven Kirsch, founder and chairman, Infoseek
- Jay Marshall, principal, Jay Alix & Associates
- Teresa McBride, CEO, McBride Associates
- Kim Pendergast, founder and president, the Pendergast Group
- John W. Rogers, president, Ariel Mutual Funds

Without benefit of a crystal ball, what can be said about such young people? Clearly, the performance of leaders can't be evaluated adequately at the take-off point—or even at the apogees—of their careers. Too many promising leaders start off like rockets—only to flare out in midcourse. Others, with less apparent potential, start more slowly but, by the touch-down of their careers, will have compiled enviable leadership records. So who knows who tomorrow's leaders will be?

Nevertheless, there is something one *can* say with certainty about the Crown Fellows listed above: they all are diligently preparing themselves to assume greater leadership responsibilities. They gather three times a year to engage in deep discussions about the leadership of others (and about their own experiences). They go back in history and philosophy to reflect on the works of Plato, Sophocles, Hobbes, Machiavelli, and, especially, Aristotle to discern the timeless lessons of leadership. They view the film *Gandhi* and discuss its relevance for today's business leaders. They read and discuss business cases relating to ABB and Percy Barnevik, GE and Jack Welch, Herman Miller and Max DePree, and SAS and Jan Carlzon—exploring the pluses and minuses of the experiences of each. And then they each accept the personal responsibility to initiate a community project under the mentorship of more experienced leaders. Finally, they discuss their leadership failures, as well as their successes, with their fellows in order to learn from their collective insights.

So keep an eye on the young men and women listed above. Given their potential, dedication, and careful preparation, there's a high probability that their careers will be profiled in the next generation of leadership books.

Tough Guys

O f course, you can also succeed by doing the *opposite* of what is described in these pages!

For example, any basketball fan can cite examples of successful "take-charge" coaches who listen to no one's counsel but their own, who bark orders ("It's my way or the highway"), and who put their own careers above the interests of players (and fans). Pat Riley and Larry Brown are two examples of narcissistic, no-nonsense NBA coaches who have enviable win-loss ratios.

As a counterexample, Phil Jackson is an "invisible leader" who, by the example of his own selfless, thoughtful behavior, helped the Chicago Bulls's notoriously egotistical players "embrace a vision in which the group imperative takes precedence over individual glory." Larry Bird is another self-effacing coach who treats his players with respect by listening to their individual needs, letting them make mistakes, and helping them draw useful lessons from bad experiences. In Bird's first season as an NBA coach, his Indiana Pacers were behind by a point in an exhibition against the Dallas

Mavericks, who had possession of the ball with less than a minute remaining in the game. George Vecsey describes the scene:

> During a time-out, the rookie coach was telling the Pacers to stop the Mavericks, and then run a set play. Reggie Miller, just trying to be helpful, suggested a play that ended with his number.
>
> Some expensively clothed control freaks would have leaped up and down like a little boy on a pogo stick and screamed that they were in charge. Instead, Larry Bird calmly gave Miller a "tell-you-what" proposition. If Miller could come up with a stop, he could run his own play.
>
> Miller, who is not known for his defense, helped stop the Mavericks, and then rushed down court and swished a three-pointer that put the Pacers ahead to stay.

Where did Bird learn to lead like that? Cynics will say, "That's just who Larry Bird is." Although that is partly true, it ignores the fact that Bird learned from experience, beginning with his freshman year as a player under the University of Indiana's Bobby Knight, a legendary player abuser. Firsthand, Bird saw that the thin-skinned Knight tolerated guff from no one, yet nonetheless felt it was his right to dish it out to everyone. Bird transferred to Indiana State at the end of his first year. He seems to have concluded that it is best to treat people as you would have them treat you.

Over the years, Knight, Riley, and Brown have egotistically screamed their ways to some of the best records in basketball. Doing pretty much the opposite,

Bird and Jackson have been equally successful. Ergo, you can win either way. So the choice is clear. You must decide how you want to be seen as a leader and how you want to see yourself in the mirror. It's up to you.

Resources: *Phil Jackson, *Sacred Hoops* (New York: Hyperion, 1995).
George Vecsey "Larry Bird Almost Runs a Democracy," *New York Times,* sports section, May 13, 1998.

Townsend, Robert

It is often said that Peter Drucker invented management; if so, the late Robert Townsend invented leadership. It was Townsend who, in the 1960s, first made Avis "Try Harder" and then wrote the 1970 bestseller *Up the Organization* to help other CEOs stop their own corporations "from stifling people and strangling profits." His gutsy path breaking—in both practice and theory—would radically change the roles of those who subsequently occupied the executive suites of large corporations. (In case you were wondering, I copied this crazy, alphabetical system of chapter organization from Bob's book as a tribute to the man and his work.)

Prior to Townsend's transformation of Avis, Fortune 500 companies had been headed, variously, by entrepreneurs, inventors, financial geniuses, managers, bureaucrats, men in gray flannel suits, crown princes, dictators, petty satraps, and unimaginative combinations of the above. But Townsend was the first true, modern corporate *leader* (def: one who manifests vision, integrity, and courage in a consistent pattern of behavior that inspires trust, motivation, and responsibility on the part of followers who, in turn, become leaders themselves).

Townsend's disciples have led many companies, including at least three remarkable start-ups that I'm personally familiar with: CEO Gordon Forward introduced at Chapparal Steel Townsendian "management by adultery" (a previously X-rated concept in which Forward treated his employees like adults and then got out of the way as they set productivity records); Radica Games's CEO Bob Davids predicated his leadership philosophy on two simple Townsend commandments ("Don't con anybody—including yourself," and "Treat people with respect") and went on to create a $150 million company from scratch by becoming a toy-industry leader in technical design; and Jacques Raiman, CEO of the GSI Corporation in the 1980s, led France into the computer age with a breakthrough philosophy of bureaucracy bashing and employee involvement. When asked where he had learned to lead in such a non-Gallic way, Raiman shocked French friends by reaching into his pocket and pulling out a dog-eared first edition of *Up the Organization* (in English, no less). *Quel horreur!*

Townsend became a role model for many leaders because they responded to his candor, spontaneity, and integrity. When they met Bob they understood why it makes sense to treat people the way you would want to be treated if you were in their shoes. He never engaged in Machiavellian machination or manipulation (he treated everyone as an end, never as a means), and he was free of the hubris that afflicts too many CEOs. Townsend always said "we" and never engaged in the pathetic craving for credit, adulation, and center stage that often characterizes executive behavior.

Townsend was probably the funniest CEO who ever made big bucks in big business (admittedly, CEOs aren't bred to maximize the wit gene—but he was funny even compared with those in such clownish fields as law, politics, and journalism). Because he directed barbed advice at the powerful, he sometimes was not well received on the Chautauqua circuit, where the rule of thumb was the Eleventh Commandment: *never speak ill of those who pay the bill.* Townsend refused to kiss up: "Directors are usually the friends of the chief executive put there to keep him safely in office," he said, sticking a finger in the eye of the indolently powerful. Thus, "be sure to serve cocktails and a heavy lunch before the [board] meeting. At least one of the older directors will fall asleep (literally) at the meeting and the consequent embarrassment will make everyone eager to get the whole mess over as soon as possible."

Humor aside, Townsend was appalled by the yes-men and (later) yes-women who dominated U.S. boardrooms, and he was one of the first to promote shareholder advocacy among outside directors. Anticipating Jack Welch, Townsend had disdain for CEOs who sat on other boards: "No outside directorships and trusteeships for the chief executive. . . . You can't even run your own company, dummy." And he castigated dilettantish professional directors who sit on twelve boards and contribute to none. Heresy!

In addition, Townsend was the first corporate chief to practice what is just now being preached in the best-led corporations: no reserved parking spaces, no org. charts, no job descriptions, no short-term pandering to Wall Street, no company planes, no golf-club memberships. On the positive side: stock options for everybody, honesty as the best policy, reinvestment for the long haul, rewards for performance, commitment to product (service) quality, true delegation, encouragement of healthy dissent, and, above all, the virtue of putting customers first. You heard it right: he practiced all the above *in the 1960s*.

Townsend hated bureaucracy and bloated central headquarters. His advice: "Fire the P.R. Department." Ditto the law, purchasing, and other staffs headed by "V.P.'s of." "Fire the Personnel Department," he said most famously, not only because those supernumeraries produce little at great expense but, more important, because no significant contribution to corporate excellence had ever been led by an H.R. department. So why not get rid of it? Sacrilege!

OK, so Townsend was a bit controversial. But that's a characteristic of great leadership, and Bob didn't back down when critics turned up the heat. He didn't care what people thought about him personally; what he cared about was creating an organization that was both profitable and an exciting place to work. In short, Bob changed people's lives by involving and energizing them in the process of creating a better future for their organizations. Bob changed lives by giving people the courage of their convictions.

In March 1970, fresh out of grad school and working at my first real job, I found myself suffering from chronic management heartburn. (See **X**-Factor.) Searching for a cure, I had tried *everything*—deep breathing, Tums, reciting Bible verses—but nothing worked. Then, on one extended lunch-time foray, by chance I picked up a hot-off-the-press copy of Townsend's book. I took three quick doses and felt better immediately.

Emboldened, I went to my boss and told him how we, too, could become an innovative, productive organization where people would actually enjoy coming to work. In measured tones, he explained this would occur only over my dead body (*my* body, mind you, not his). I took the hint, cleared off my desk, descended forty-eight floors to street level, and never went back. Ever since, whenever I've felt a case of organizational blues coming on, I've dug into *Up the Organization* for a booster shot of uncommon common sense.

Resource: *Robert Townsend, *Up the Organization* (New York: Knopf, 1970). A version of this chapter originally appeared in *Across the Board*.

Training
(Why It Isn't a Useful Part of Leadership Development)

Corporations in the United States spend gazillions on in-house leadership training. It amounts to well-intentioned money going down the drain. This wasted money—wasted opportunity, really—derives from a fundamental misunderstanding in the minds of those in charge of corporate executive development: *they confuse training with education.* Although both are subcategories of the more generic notion of learning, they are not, as the H.R. folks would have it, synonymous.

Can executives be *trained* to be leaders? To answer that question, we should draw a clear distinction between training and education. *Training,* according to Webster, means "forming habits of thought and behavior by discipline and instruction." This process is applied, it is practical, and the results are immediate. Training has to do with right and wrong—right and wrong answers, right and wrong behavior. It has to do with facts, with a set body of information, with how-tos and how-to-dos. It is appropriate for routine and repetitive tasks. Training is useful when the right outcome is known in advance by a trainer, who can tell whether she or he has succeeded when the trainee either (a) answers a question correctly or (b) behaves appropriately.

Because clear outcomes are identifiable at the beginning of a training process, precise lesson plans can be developed, and the outcomes can be measured. *McDonald's Hamburger U. trains people to make Big Macs the right way.*

Education, again according to Webster, means "to develop the faculties and powers of a person." The word comes from the Latin root of the word *educe,* or draw out. It is, therefore, a maieutic, or Socratic, process. Education is not immediately practical. It is designed to develop the capacity to learn. That is why it is often said that the most important thing one learns in school is how to learn. We learn to ask fundamental questions and to challenge assumptions. The process, when done right, equips us to explore issues and ideas from multiple perspectives. Thus, it broadens us. It is not about learning right answers; it is about learning how to ask the right questions in order that one can become innovative, creative, and responsive to change. It is developmental. *A liberal arts college educates students so they will be equipped to learn throughout their lives.*

There is danger in equating the two types of learning. Training has to do with indoctrination, while education encourages the challenging of established ideas. Thus, although one might want to indoctrinate the kids who flip burgers at Mickey D's, one presumably wants the top management team of McDonald's to think creatively about new markets, new strategies, and new opportunities. Those cognitive skills cannot be acquired through training.

Turning from the individual to the organization, nearly everyone today agrees that continuous learning is requisite for corporate success. Great companies are characterized by their habitual reflection on experience—followed by institutionalized modifications in organizational behavior. Such adaptive "learning organizations" are accurately said to cope most effectively with change. *Ergo, trainers develop programs to help executives learn to cope with change.* But that prescription doesn't follow.

People can't be trained to respond creatively to a constantly changing environment (although it is possible to train them to cope with the effects of a single change). Training programs don't create learning cultures because linking the modifier *change* to the noun *training* creates little more than an oxymoron. Training—which, by definition, assumes a single right answer—is antithetical to the collective flexibility of mind and habit required to cope with change. And although they may deny it, corporate trainers unconsciously assume a single, right outcome and favor pedagogical methods (lectures, simulations, games, outdoor "ropes and rocks") the results of which are predictable and controllable. Doubtless, such methods are perfectly appropriate for some important behavioral changes. For example, Denny's used training appropriately to change the unconscious racist behavior of its restaurant employees.

Moreover, it is unfair to single out corporate trainers for failing to understand the difference between training and education. Indeed, so-called schools of education, ironically, teach only methods of training. Even at the university level, training too often takes precedence over education. For example, most professors of biogenetics feel they have succeeded if their students acquire a body of facts and the ability to apply them. These professors check how well their students have done through true-false and multiple-choice tests. That's training. In contrast, Dr. David Eisenberg of UCLA gives his undergraduates in biogenetics an intriguing term project: he has them identify a major source of controversy in the field, read the published articles on both sides, and then write a critical review of the articles, explaining why each side makes its respective claims and evaluating the merit of the various arguments. *That* is education.

In the field of business, most U.S. instructors who deal with Asia teach "how-to-do-business" courses about China, Japan, or wherever. They feel they have succeeded if their instructees know the ins and outs of an Asian country's bureaucracy, laws, customs, financial institutions, and the like. That's training. In contrast, Harvard professor Tu Wei-ming teaches an executive seminar in which participants read and discuss core philosophical texts from Asia and the West. At the end of his seminar, I've heard U.S. executives say, "Now I understand how Asians think," and Asian executives say, "Now I understand how Westerners think." *That* is education.

Appropriate methods for the education of leaders include: reading widely, confronting diverse opinions and values, analyzing history, participating in seminar and case discussions, and action learning (reflecting on experience). These broadening approaches develop the habits of mind that are essential for leadership: specifically, the ability to see issues from multiple perspectives and, thus, to create visions and strategies that accommodate and encompass the different values, aspirations, and points of view of followers. In sharp contrast is training, which has no useful role in leadership development because it is narrowing in both practice and intent.

Transforming Leadership

James Houghton got to be CEO of Corning the old-fashioned way: he inherited the job. Because leadership ability isn't also inheritable, his prospects for success were, statistically speaking, worse than average. Whereas most people who make it to the executive suites of Fortune 500 companies do so by dint of meritocratic competition, in contrast, Houghton fell into a position for which he was relatively ill prepared and inexperienced. Given that inauspicious beginning, his subsequent career is particularly inspirational because Houghton became one of the most impressive "transforming leaders" of the last two decades of the twentieth century. As defined by James MacGregor Burns, transforming leaders address the true needs of followers, give them a vision of a future that satisfies those needs, and then engage them in the process of achieving the vision. That's what Houghton did over the course of a decade at Corning.

I have never met James Houghton. However, for over eight years, I studied his career carefully and evaluated his performance by means of triangulation: my sources of information were individuals who worked for Corning in executive, managerial and employee positions; people who had served on Corning's board (and as financial analysts specializing in Corning); and scholars, consultants, and journalists who, professionally, studied the company firsthand and observed Houghton's career.

Remarkably, they almost all came to a similar conclusion: Jamie Houghton was an unlikely prospect who turned himself into a truly effective leader. They speculate that what Houghton had going for him (besides a good liberal arts education) was an uncommon willingness to learn from experience, to listen to and to trust others, and to work hard and persistently to achieve his aspirations for the company founded by his great-great-grandfather.

When Houghton became CEO in 1983, Corning was suffering from years of mismanagement and neglect. It had poor labor relations, outmoded plants and technology, declining market share, and it faced increasingly tough foreign competition. Less than a decade later, the company was producing new, high-quality products, thanks to a motivated workforce, and was well positioned to be a profitable player in the emerging global economy. Here are some of the things Houghton and his leadership team did to create that transformation.

He Formed a Team. One of Houghton's first acts was to assemble a six-person leadership team (dubbed "the six-pack") of managers who shared his belief that Corning needed to change if it were to survive.

The Team Created a Vision. The six-pack identified a new strategic direction for Corning. Then they affirmed a set of values that were consistent with, and instrumental to, the achievement of that vision. And they identified "quality" as the unifying theme for a companywide process designed to change the culture, behavior, and practices of everyone in the firm.

The Team Changed Its Own Behavior. Because they were inexperienced, the six-pack began by making all the classical errors associated with failed change efforts: they announced a "program" and then sat back expecting it to be implemented; they failed to fully engage workers, the union, and middle management; they delegated the leadership of change while devoting their own efforts to their usual managerial tasks; and they continued Corning's tradition of command-and-control management. Not surprisingly, the quality program went nowhere and remained stuck on square one until, in the midst of considerable frustration, Jamie Houghton finally got it. He realized that *he* would have to lead the change, that he and the team would have to involve others in the effort, and that they would have to win over skeptics and resisters by giving them a real stake in the process. Jamie, who had been spending about a third of his time on the quality initiative, then put aside all the nonessential activities that unproductively devour the day of an executive and devoted 100 percent of his time to leading change at Corning.

The Team Created an Architecture for Change. Houghton and the six-pack concluded that their role was to create the conditions under which others could effectively identify and implement the needed changes. This was easier said than done. Resistance to change was rampant in light of Corning's history of adversarial labor relations. Why should the unionized workforce accept the responsibility to help management achieve *its* goals? Why should workers trust a management that had been repeatedly untrustworthy in the past?

But Jamie proved to be a different breed of cat from his predecessors in the executive suite. He patiently hung in during the fray, delivering the same thoughtful message, building his credibility through consistency, and demonstrating that he wasn't going away until the workers finally listened with open minds. (See

Repetition, Repetition, Repetition . . . .) Finally, the workers started to hear his message: the best way to ensure their jobs in the future was for *them* to improve product quality and the overall efficiency of Corning's operations. Top management would provide the workers with objectives, resources, training, and support; in exchange, the workers would find the most efficient ways to provide the highest-quality products in the industry. To sweeten the pot, the company agreed to share financial gains with the workers.

They Established Boundaries. In essence, Jamie and the six-pack told the workers that they had authority to make whatever changes were necessary in order to achieve their quality goals. Still, the workers balked. Based on past experience, they doubted that Jamie meant it when he talked about empowering them. "Come on," they said, "tell us the truth: how much authority do we have?" It was at this point that Jamie earned his spurs as a leader. He told the workers that they had full authority within the confines of each plant to make whatever decisions and whatever changes in organization, technology, and governance *they* felt were necessary. For instance, they could set their own staffing levels—even reduce the authority and number of managers and supervisors in a plant! But he made it clear that he wasn't writing them a blank check. They were *not* empowered to: act in ways that violated the basic values of Corning; move outside the scope of the overall corporate strategy and objectives (for example, they couldn't choose to drop the glass business and make, say, surfboards); engage in top-management concerns (for example, they couldn't issue their own financial paper); or make decisions that affected other Corning operations without their full concurrence. "Wow," the workers said, "this guy is a straight shooter. He means business." (See **A**BB's Benchstrength.)

He Redefined Leadership. Because the transformation of Corning required the active involvement of everyone down the line, it became clear to Houghton that the major obstacle in the way of that happening was the prevalent philosophy of leadership in the company (and, in fact, in industry in general). "We have traditionally viewed leaders as heroes who came forward at a time of crisis to resolve a problem," he wrote in 1992. "But this view stresses the short term and assures the powerlessness of those being led." Because his goal was, in effect, to put the burden of change on the followers, he resolved that he, the six-pack, and every other leader in Corning would have to abandon the traditional view of the leader as font of all wisdom and adopt, instead, a philosophy of transforming leadership:

> The true spirit of leadership is the spirit that is not sure it is always right. Leaders who are not too sure they are right are leaders who listen. Leadership is about performance over time, not charisma—about responsibility, not privilege. It is about personal integrity and a strong belief in team play. . . .
>
> Which points to one more element of leadership: developing strong subordinates and potential successors and staying out of their way. Companies can no longer afford leadership by the few. If organizations are to move ahead and not just play catch-up, every employee must become a responsible leader. . . .
>
> Employees must have responsibility and the power that goes with it; anything less leads to cynicism and skepticism—and nothing is more demoralizing for employees than to find their skepticism justified.

He Persisted. For nearly a decade, Houghton practiced what he preached. And he said the same things over and over again until he was blue in the face, and until everyone finally got the message. (See **R**epetition, Repetition, Repetition . . . .) Whenever there was pressure from the board or Wall Street to cut back on the company's expensive quality training program, he drew a line in the sand and said that training was integral to the long-term change effort. In so doing, he reinforced his commitment to his principles in the eyes of Corning's workforce. Through thick and thin he repeated his message, reaffirmed his commitment to change, and behaved consistently with his redefinition of leadership.

With each passing year he was able to report to Corning employees and shareholders that the company's quality, productivity, competitiveness, and profitability were improving. However, in his last report to the shareholders, in 1993, he noted that Corning's competitors had enhanced greatly their ability to move quickly and to change their own practices. He warned that those new challenges would require renewed effort. . . . And then disaster struck. While attending a conference in Williamsburg, Virginia, Houghton stepped off a curb and was hit by a careless taxi driver. Because he was never able to return fully to active leadership of Corning, we don't know what Jamie would have done to meet the new challenges he had identified.

Resources: *James MacGregor Burns, *Leadership* (New York: HarperCollins, 1978).
*James Houghton, "Leadership's Challenge: The New Agenda for the '90s," *Planning Review,*
September/October 1992.

Transformations, Continued
(and Continual)

When last we saw James Houghton (see Transforming Leadership), he had just had a terrible accident that would leave him too weakened physically to fully assume Corning's leadership. About that same time, Houghton's quality orientation had begun to show signs that it would be an insufficient response to the emerging challenges of the fast-growing markets Corning was entering—optical fibers, life sciences, and other high-tech business that were taking the company far afield from the housewares that had been its primary business a decade earlier (when Jamie became CEO).

Worse yet, in 1993 Corning was hit with an enormous one-time charge to cover legal settlements related to the (separately managed) Dow Corning's ill-fated silicon breast implants. As luck would have it, all of the above conspired to come together in the same year, leaving the company unable to meet its earnings target for the first time under Houghton's leadership.

Jamie's response was to kick himself upstairs to the chairman's post and to name a member of the six-pack, Roger Ackerman, as Corning's CEO. Houghton charged Ackerman not only with turning around the immediate financial situation but also with comprehensively changing Corning's culture to meet the realities of its new markets, and energizing the company to create the ongoing capabilities necessary to drive profitable growth in the future.

Note that Houghton did *not* require Ackerman to either preserve or justify his ten-year quality emphasis. Instead, whereas Houghton's change effort had focused *vertically* on quality improvement within each of the company's discrete business units, Ackerman's would be a comprehensive, integrated approach that encouraged the *horizontal* flow of information and cooperation across organizational boundaries. In other words, Houghton's efforts focused on gaining organizational alignment, whereas Ackerman's were directed more toward building adaptability.

That doesn't mean Ackerman threw out the past or ignored all Jamie had accomplished. Rather, he built on that sound foundation. In his "Corning Competes" initiative, Ackerman preserved the basic values of the company: for example, in setting a numerical target of reducing operational costs by $450 million over three years, he stipulated that this must occur without radical downsizing, which would have a negative impact on the employment and economy in Corning, New York (the company town).

Although Houghton's health would force him to retire before Corning Competes was very far along, he supported Ackerman's efforts to change key aspects of the Corning culture—to speed up decision making, to create greater cost consciousness, and to share best practices.

Ackerman's approach to the process of change was somewhat different from Houghton's. In order to create the necessary cross-functional mind-set for horizontal change, Ackerman co-located Corning Competes team members in what would become known as the Donut Factory (it was housed next to a Dunkin' Donuts outlet on Corning's Main Street). The mission of the teams was "to engage the organization and challenge it to seek new ways of conducting business." In the absence of a real crisis (the breast-implant tragedy was not of Corning Inc.'s making), Ackerman's challenge was not only to get people to act but, first, to get them to see the need for action.

Because Ackerman believed that rigorous analytical content was a prerequisite for effective action, in Phase 1 of Corning Competes several teams were assigned to work full time to create an objective, unassailable case for change. Ackerman describes Corning Competes' four phases: "Using an analytical, hypothesis-driven approach, the Phase 1 teams scanned the entire enterprise to find opportunities for improvement that would have the highest impact. . . . After the opportunities were identified, follow-up teams were established to drive the process forward. Moving from Phase 2 to Phase 3 involved the development of specific and quantifiable improvement opportunities and the preparation of implementation plans. Phase 4, the final step, was to implement and track results."

During all four phases, Ackerman and other members of Corning's top management played the central role of communicating the effort to all levels of the company:

> Going after the hearts and minds of Corning's vital constituencies—employees, suppliers and customers—involved everything from town meetings and monthly Corning Competes bulletins to focus groups, surveys and the establishment of a 1-800 line. The goal of this communication process was to reach every employee on a regular basis with a consistent message. There was a focus on building in a feedback loop, so employees could express anxieties about the process. This resulted in "Headlines in a Hurry," an electronic message center that responded to employee questions, typically within 72 hours. Senior

management was heavily involved throughout the process, clearly demonstrating that change started at the top of the organization.

In addition to communication, top management's role included setting stretch goals and then holding people accountable for results. *But the actual work of change was done by the teams.* In all, some three hundred Corning people from the shop floor to the boardroom spent time at the Donut Factory. This level of participation was necessary to ensure that the recommendations of the Corning Competes teams were sufficiently owned by the line organizations who would be responsible for implementing them. The most successful of such initiatives, according to Ackerman, were ones in which a product champion emerged who assumed responsibility to see that recommendations were implemented: "The ability to drive change often comes down to a simple yet resolutely abstract concept—leadership."

In fact, phalanxes of leaders were needed "to ask questions, follow-up, measure, and reward new behaviors," according to Norm Garrity, president of Corning Technologies. Such leaders let it be known to line managers that "they wouldn't go away" until the operational people implemented the necessary changes. Such adamant persistence paid off: Corning Competes exceeded its cost-reduction targets in each of the first three years of the program. Moreover, the effort institutionalized new behaviors across the organization.

Checking in at Corning five years after the first teams had gathered at the Donut Factory, one would have found that the change process was not over. In fact, according to Ackerman, it should never be finished because, from the outset, the intent was to create organizational agility and the capacity to engage in continuous improvement. For example, Ackerman has since launched a globalization team charged with developing Corning's ability to capitalize quickly on emerging opportunities around the world.

In the final analysis, then, Jamie Houghton's career didn't have a formal second act; instead, it had a knockout first act that has enabled his successor to keep on going and going . . .

Resource: *Roger G. Ackerman and Gary L. Neilson, "Partnering for Results: A Case Study of Re-engineering the Corning Way," *Strategy & Business,* no. 3, 1996.

Trust

Trust is the glue that binds people together in groups. Whenever followers are asked what they require of leaders, trust is almost always at the top of the list. But leaders can't provide trust directly to followers. The hitch is that trust is an outcome of leadership actions and behavior: Hence, leaders can't *do* trust.

Fortunately, it is no deep secret what leaders need to do indirectly to foster a climate of trust. When leaders are candid, open, consistent, and predictable in their dealings with followers, the result will almost always be a condition of trust. Fundamentally, trust is the consequence of honesty and truth telling. It follows that leaders who tell the truth will, ipso facto, tell everyone the same thing. This constancy allows followers to act with the assurance that the rules of the game won't suddenly change and that they will not be treated arbitrarily. Given that assurance, followers become more willing to stick their necks out, make an extra effort, and put themselves on the line to help leaders achieve organizational goals.

Unfortunately, such consistency is difficult for many leaders to maintain because it requires the relatively elusive trait of integrity. Leaders have integrity when they mean what they say and practice what they preach. For this to happen leaders must first know what they believe, which means they must know themselves. To leaders who know themselves, integrity comes naturally. For example, Gandhi never had to ask of himself, "Now, just what is it that I believe in?" And he never had to remind himself what he had last said to this or that person. As the old saying goes, "If you tell the truth, you never have to remember what you said."

Yet the creation of trust isn't simply a process internal to the leader, and it requires even more of leaders than integrity. In addition, trust has an external dimension manifested in the behavior of leaders toward followers: when leaders treat followers with respect, followers respond with trust. In practice, leaders show their respect for followers by always treating them as ends in themselves—that is, leaders never treat followers as the means to achieve their own ego or power goals or even to achieve the legitimate goals of the organization.

Leaders demonstrate their respect for followers by what they do: by telling them the truth, by never using them or manipulating them, and by including them in decision-making processes that affect their well-being. Such inclusion, of course, is the most difficult aspect of leadership. Indeed, most leaders say that it is hard, if not impossible, always to practice inclusion. But always it must be because, as the managing director of Britain's Coleman's Ltd. explains, "In the absence of trust, all ambiguous behavior is viewed with suspicion. And, all behavior is ambiguous!" That's why the failure to include people is the second most common source of mistrust in organizations, close behind the failure of leaders to tell the truth consistently.

The prevailing ideology of leadership—contingency theory—unwittingly leads to the creation of mistrust because it encourages leaders to shift course arbitrarily and to do whatever they think is expedient in order to achieve their goals, including going back on their word. To renege on one's word may seem necessary to some leaders, but in the eyes of followers it is always viewed as a betrayal of trust.

Trust must be earned. And it is hard to earn, easy to lose, and, once lost, nearly impossible to regain. That is why there are so many would-be leaders but so few successful ones.

Resources: *J. M. Kouzes and B. Z. Posner, *The Leadership Challenge* (San Francisco: Jossey-Bass, 1995). *J. M. Kouzes and B. Z. Posner, *Credibility* (San Francisco: Jossey-Bass, 1993).

LEADERSHIP
A to Z

Up and Out
(and Sideways)

Most leaders devote their efforts downward in their organizations, seeking to create followers among their subordinates. In addition, great leaders accept responsibility for leading their peers, leading outside constituencies, and even leading those above them.

While Gandhi was busy unifying the Indian masses, he also spent enormous energy teaching his peers in the Congress Party how to lead, and, moreover, he devoted considerable time to gaining support for his cause among British and other foreign opinion leaders and publics. Likewise, Pope John Paul II spends the majority of his time tending his flock of faithful Catholics—but what makes him a true leader in the eyes of the world is his willingness to exert his moral authority to influence the behavior of heads of state, even if they are Protestant, Moslem, or anti-Christian Communists. Indeed, Pope Pius XII's failure in the 1940s to condemn Hitler and the extermination of millions of non-Catholics is, today, widely viewed as a gross abnegation of the moral responsibilities of leadership.

To be truly effective, the CEO of even a petroleum company has to be willing to lead upward, outward, and sideways. David Law-Smith is CEO of CALTEX, the world's oldest and most successful corporate joint venture (it is owned by Texaco and Chevron). CALTEX is perhaps the most truly global corporation, with operations in over fifty countries (none in North America, which is why you may not have heard of this $5 billion behemoth).

Because most of CALTEX's operations are in the developing countries of Africa and Asia—and because the oil business is invariably considered to be a "national interest"—Law-Smith must be a statesman in addition to being a businessman. Moreover, because he has built a reputation as a thoughtful, articulate, straight shooter, he is in demand to serve as an industry spokesman at such prestigious international forums as Davos, the Aspen Institute, and Oxford Analytica's annual conference.

Law-Smith has a highly developed sense of his leadership role vis-à-vis CALTEX's numerous and varied constituencies—employees, governments, joint-venture partners, environmentalists, customers, suppliers, industry groups, and, of course, shareholders. Consequently, he has to think through his priorities carefully or his efforts will be spread so thin that he will be effective with none of those stakeholders. His rule of thumb is to be involved only in activities that require the authority of the CEO—and to delegate everything else.

For example, he created a task force to completely reorganize CALTEX's operations worldwide; a major goal is to put more managerial responsibility in the hands of foreign nationals from developing countries. Law-Smith initiated this effort, encouraged it, and supported it, but he was not involved in doing it. This major transformation of CALTEX's culture was accomplished with impressive speed and effectiveness, which was due, in no small part, to Law-Smith's holding the people involved accountable for making timely decisions. But *he* didn't make those decisions. Instead, he devoted his own energies to those things that his subordinates could not do.

Thus, he saw early on that the cultural change wouldn't take hold, or last, if it were not reinforced by a complete rehaul of the corporation's compensation and governance systems. Because that was a board decision, Law-Smith took the lead to make the case, to persuade and educate CALTEX's board about the necessity for change—and he assumed full responsibility for the consequences. In sum, because David Law-Smith is so effective leading up, out, and sideways, his people are more effective in their efforts to lead change down through the organization.

One of the many myths of leadership is that leaders stand at the pinnacle of authority and, thus, are accountable to no one. In truth, with the exception of dictators (who, by definition, aren't leaders) everybody is ultimately responsible to somebody. We all have a boss (in the case of the U.S. president that particular boss is the people) or someone or some body of people to whom we must report. In most organizations, the highest body is usually a board of directors or trustees.

Yet, the relationship of CEOs to their boards is not a simple, direct, reporting arrangement. Boards need leadership, too, and that leadership often must come, at least to a degree, from the president or CEO who, paradoxically, also reports to them. Given the complexity of having to lead those who evaluate them, many CEOs take the cowardly way out and abdicate their responsibility to fully inform, challenge, and shape the thinking of their boards. But in the final reckoning, every effective leader—CEOs, presidents, division heads, supervisors, you, and I—must assume the responsibility of leading those to whom we report. All leaders must educate their superiors. And that's a much tougher task than issuing orders to subordinates.

Resource: *Cyrus Friedheim, *The Trillion-Dollar Enterprise* (New York: Perseus, 1999).

LEADERSHIP
A to Z

Vision

Vision in German is cloud cuckoo land. I am interested in staying down to earth.
—Helmut Schmidt

The easiest part of leadership is the "vision thing." Creating a vision is simply the act of visualizing better conditions or circumstances than exist at present. George Bush's embarrassing shortcomings in this department notwithstanding, most people have a vision of what their country or organization could, and should, look like in the future. In the early 1970s, I interviewed men and women who worked in General Motors auto-assembly plants and was surprised to learn that they all had visions of a more productive GM—one in which labor and management would cooperate in order to make high-quality cars. They could even flesh out how both workers and managers would have to change their behavior and practices in order to achieve the vision. What struck me as incredible was that, in contrast, GM's top executives seemed totally incapable of imagining anything other than the miserable labor relations that existed at the time.

Executives, I have since learned, unnecessarily work themselves up into a lather over the issue of vision creation. Perhaps because management training doesn't encourage creativity, executives assume they aren't adept at feats of imagination. Over the years, I have asked managers to rank order what they consider to be the hardest things for them to change in their organizations. Vision always makes the top of the list. Yet, in actual practice, vision is the easiest thing to change (most successful transformation efforts devote, at most, a few weeks to vision creation—but *years* to changing behavior to get alignment with the vision):

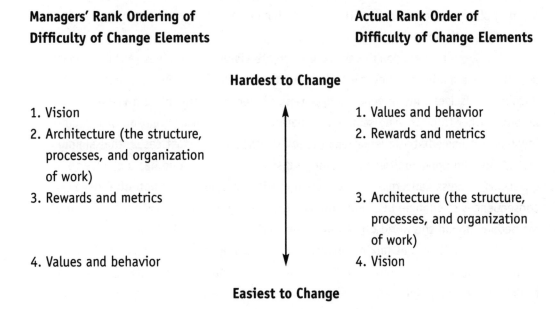

Managers' Rank Ordering of Difficulty of Change Elements	Actual Rank Order of Difficulty of Change Elements

Hardest to Change

1. Vision	1. Values and behavior
2. Architecture (the structure, processes, and organization of work)	2. Rewards and metrics
3. Rewards and metrics	3. Architecture (the structure, processes, and organization of work)
4. Values and behavior	4. Vision

Easiest to Change

Given how difficult they find the act of vision creation, isn't it odd that few leaders ever admit to *not* having one? Still, we can appreciate that it would be hard to be a leader and not have at least some inkling about what the organization would look like if it were functioning more effectively. From the executives' perspective, then, the problem is not their own lack of vision but, rather, the failure of others to support that vision. Well, there are visions . . . and then there are visions.

A robust vision mobilizes appropriate behavior. It uses memorable, simple concepts that make clear what needs to be different about tomorrow. It describes the distinctive competencies needed to deliver on the desired end state (for example, "Here's what we have to do differently in order to succeed"). Often, a vision will make choices clear by making the case for change as either an opportunity or a burning platform (for example, "If we don't change in this way, the company won't survive"). That's not asking for much, is it?

Leaders don't even have to create visions themselves (although many do). But, at a minimum, they must initiate a process for developing a vision and then engage themselves fully in generating buy-in. Shared commitment to a vision can be built either through wide-scale participation in the act of its creation or through involvement immediately thereafter in its dissemination. In most cases, that simply means creating opportunities for thorough discussion so everyone has a chance to ask questions, express concerns, and deal openly with anxieties about potential negative consequences of change. BP's John Browne did this by linking up twenty thousand of his people around the world on PCs in an interactive visioning exercise.

We're not talking quantum mechanics here. This is simple stuff—so simple that many leaders gloss over the basics. For example, by definition, vision has to do with "seeing, sight, and sensing with the eyes." Recognizing that simple fact, effective leaders make their visions, well, *visual*. Remember Ronald Reagan's budget message when he explained that a trillion bucks amounts to a stack of dough as high as the Empire State building? By using that visual reference, he got Americans to *see* that federal spending amounts to real money! In so doing, he changed the terms of the national debate and, for the first time, created a majority in support of lower taxes. It was his most effective moment as a leader.

As part of an ongoing effort to change the culture of the benefits division of the Veterans Administration (the $23 billion in benefits the VA administers annually stacks up at least as high as the Flatiron Building), Undersecretary Joe Thompson first conveyed his vision in the form of a video. Thompson and his management team identified the bureaucratic behavior that would have to change in order for the VA to provide prompt, efficient, and respectful service to veterans; then, they found clips from old movies in which the opposite of such behavior was humorously portrayed. Splicing short segments together from films by the likes of the Marx Brothers, Mel Brooks, Monty Python, and John Belushi, Thompson created an engaging way to show his people visually that what they were doing was unacceptable. Because this serious message was delivered in a funny context, VA employees were able to internalize it without being insulted. From that point, an open dialogue ensued in which employees freely discussed what they would have to do to change. (See **G**uvmint Work.)

When Boeing's Alan Mulally took charge of the postmerger integration of the aerospace divisions of the Boeing, Rockwell, and McDonnell-Douglas companies, he decided that the new organization's vision should be entirely visual (in other words, *no words!*). He flipped through documents from all three companies, cut out pictures of artist renderings of proposed products and of technologies in development, and then pasted these in creative juxtaposition on a large piece of poster board.

At the initial meeting of the new top management team, Mulally unveiled his vision for their future. At first, they didn't get it. So he asked them to study it and to talk about it among themselves, with their teams, and with him. Then, each time it was necessary to make a presentation to Boeing's board, stockholders, Wall Street analysts, customers, or employees, Mulally would assign a different executive to explain, in his own words, what the vision meant. By the end of a year, everyone down to the shop floor could describe the vision and its significance to their work.

So vision creation is easy (but a little showmanship never hurts!).

Resource: *Burt Nanus, *Visionary Leadership* (San Francisco: Jossey-Bass, 1992).

W

LEADERSHIP
A to Z

What Leaders Do, a Checklist
(and an Index)

We're to that place in the alphabet where it's time to recapitulate. So, in order to create followers—who, in turn, will create a high-performing, self-renewing organization—leaders must *do* the following:

I. *Set the Course*	**Primary References**
❏ Select a leadership team	pp. 117–118; 260–262
❏ Listen to followers and then identify their needs	pp. 80–82; 109–111; 170–174
❏ Generate a shared vision and values	pp. 107–108; 121–123; 300–304
❏ Build a case for change	pp. 119; 214–216; 286–290
❏ Link change to the needs of followers	pp. 96–98; 232–235; 280–285
❏ Create a sense of hope	pp. 140–141; 192–193; 230–231

II. *Change Behavior*   **Primary References**

- ❑ Challenge, stretch, and motivate   pp. 23–26; 224–227; 269–271
- ❑ Define appropriate behavior   pp. 96–98; 107–108; 114–116
- ❑ Hold people accountable   pp. 8–14; 119; 286–290
- ❑ Reward, celebrate, and reinforce
  positive behavior   pp. 15–16; 114–116; 208–211
- ❑ Punish inappropriate behavior   pp. 134–136

III. *Provide Rewards*

- ❑ Create appropriate metrics
  (focused on the essentials)   pp. 55–60; 208–211
- ❑ Set and enforce limits
  (define levels of empowerment)   pp. 8–14; 43–45; 55–57
- ❑ Reduce fear of failure and of
  risk taking   pp. 23–26; 187–190
- ❑ Reward learning, experimentation,
  and innovation   pp. 43–45; 187–190; 247–249

IV. *Communicate*

- ❑ Communicate the purpose of
  the organization   pp. 43–45; 75–77; 162–163
- ❑ Put themselves on the line
  (make a commitment)   pp. 40–42; 128; 280–285
- ❑ Coach and teach   pp. 196–198; 258–259; 276–279
- ❑ Live the values of the
  organization (practice integrity)   pp. 63–64

❑ Speak the truth consistently
(lay the groundwork for trust)   pp. 61–62; 202–205; 291–293
❑ Use appropriate symbols and
universal values   pp. 124–126; 254–255
❑ Encourage diversity of opinion   pp. 71–74

V. *Focus on Performance*

❑ Reframe organizational challenges/
redefine business reality   pp. 117–119; 208–211; 232–235
❑ Create a sense of urgency   pp. 117–119; 232–235; 247–249
❑ Link metrics to performance   pp. 58–60; 128–129; 208–211
❑ Fight complacency (energize
the organization)   pp. 92–95; 272–275

VI. *Create Appropriate Architecture*

❑ Provide resources (including
authority and power)   pp. 69–70; 187–190; 240–241
❑ Create conditions under which
others can lead   pp. 180–184; 286–290
❑ Create alignment among strategy,
structure, and processes   pp. 38–39; 129; 280–285
❑ Practice inclusion (show respect
for followers)   pp. 129–130; 137–139; 145–147
❑ Engage the middle of the
organization   pp. 96–98; 286–290

Why Leaders Won't Lead

Alas, most people in positions of titular authority lack the ambition to become true leaders. A case in point is N, the CEO of a well-known corporation, the financial performance of which is slightly above the average of Fortune 500 firms. Although N's board of directors seem as content as hogs in slop, two of his exec veeps recently approached him with a stark view of the firm's long-term future. They warned that prospects for growth were slim without a major refocusing of the company's main lines of business: if the company didn't change its strategic direction, it faced the painful fate of being nibbled to death by more agile competitors. "That's why we need to get out of business X and go into business Y in a big way," they said.

N listened intently and then asked them what, in practice, would be entailed in an effort to turn the organization around. The veeps candidly warned that the powerful heads of the traditional business lines would resist mightily any effort to redirect the corporation, and they might even make an end run to the board to make the case against "risking" change. Ergo, the only chance for success was for N to lead the transformation effort himself, perhaps by going public with a compelling case for change and then by holding everyone's feet to the fire during what promised to be a difficult implementation stage.

N weighed his options carefully. Three factors seemed relevant to him: (1) being in his early sixties, he could look forward at most to a three-year tenure in the executive suite; (2) there was probably enough inertia to avoid collapse on his watch; and (3) the odds of a successful transformation weren't as good as the near certainty of his getting embroiled in a bruising fight. Thus, he quietly decided to do nothing to upset the forces of resistance.

Unfortunately, such shirking of leadership responsibility is not that uncommon at Fortune 500 companies (even in this era of ungodly pressures to perform). Only a minority of corporate CEOs put themselves on the line to make their companies great, only a few engage in building a rich legacy for their successors, and only a minuscule number accept the responsibility to create a self-renewing organization. And, as with N, most CEOs find cogent reasons for *not* leading change, to wit:

- They don't have *time*.
- The work is *hard*.
- It is *risky* if they do act.
- They could just as easily *coast out*.
- They are *alone* at the top.
- There may not be a clear *reward* at the end.
- They don't know *what* to do.
- They don't know what *not* to do.

There are plenty of reasons for not leading, and most executives consciously or unconsciously excuse themselves from action by embracing one or more of what are, precisely, that—*excuses*. In fact, what they lack is appropriate ambition. And that is why the names of most corporate CEOs fade from the collective memory, almost on the day they retire. We remember only the leaders.

LEADERSHIP
A to Z

X-Factor

Starting at the turn of the twentieth century with the influential writings of sociologist Max Weber, scholars, managers, consultants, and just about everyone involved in large organizations tried to do without leadership—either by attempting to substitute an administrative equivalent or by simply ignoring the subject. Leadership wasn't even a part of the business school curriculum until very recently.

In 1969, when I was a wet-behind-the-ears, twenty-four-year-old consultant with McKinsey and Company, as far as I can recall the word *leadership* was never uttered. (See Townsend, Robert.)

My first assignment was on a change-management team at a large Canadian forest-products corporation. The company was in bad shape financially, even though it was favored with extensive holdings of productive timberland on vernal Vancouver Island. Our McKinsey team was composed mainly of Harvard B-School types, all conversant with the latest management methods, techniques, and theories. After much sophisticated quantitative analysis (we used big IBM computers, which, in the late sixties, was evidence that we were on the cutting edge of *everything*), the team decided that we should introduce the hottest idea of the era: management by objectives.

The concept of MBO was to break down an organization into small units, and then each part would set objectives consistent with, and supportive of, the objectives of the next layer up in the hierarchy. The idea was that if every business unit knew its small part in the overall scheme—and if it were evaluated and rewarded for meeting its objectives—the sum total would be a successful corporation that met its overarching goals. To get there, we adjusted strategies, programs, processes, and controls at each level of the Canadian company. And we created a plan for the rollout of the MBO program, which we presented to the company's executives on a hundred overhead transparencies replete with critical-path analyses, flow charts, PERT charts, GANTT charts, chart charts, and every form of schedule, matrix, program, quadrant, and formula known to management science.

It didn't work. They failed. We failed. I failed. And I couldn't figure out why. Even today, in hindsight, I think the McKinsey team did everything right technically—our theory was right, our analysis was sound, our proposed strategy was robust—and the employees of the company did everything in their power to implement our elegant scheme.

One thing I did learn quickly in the months that followed was that the experience of the Canadian company was more the rule than the exception. What I came to understand is that companies can have advantaged resources, a fine workforce, an appropriate strategy, quality products, effective marketing, sound administrative controls and procedures, *and still fail.*

For the next quarter of a century, I struggled to understand why it was that companies underperform, fail to grow, get stuck in patterns of self-defeating behavior, and do not change—even when they appear to be doing everything right according to the latest theories and frameworks advocated by first-rate business schools and consulting firms.

Put positively, the question of 1969 remains the same today: Why do some companies continually succeed when they appear to have no inherent advantages over their less successful competitors? Despite years of analysis and research, the true sources of outstanding corporate performance still remain a matter of considerable conjecture and debate. Business executives, journalists, and scholars still ask, Why is it that

- In every industry, there are only one or two truly high-performing companies, while others languish as also-rans?
- A handful of companies, year in and year out, make every list of the world's most-respected corporations, but most never make the grade?
- A few companies respond positively and rapidly to change while the majority lurch from crisis to crisis?
- Only a small number of corporations are able to remake themselves from also-rans into world leaders—and, then, rarely in the absence of a crisis?

Why? Well, dear reader, by this late stage in the alphabet I trust that you've concluded for yourself that the X-factor accounting for the success of consistently great companies is *leadership!*

Now, when I think about my Canadian experience in light of what has been summarized here (in entries A through W), the mystery of the company's late-sixties woes disappears: the problem at the lumberyard was that, to the extent anyone there thought about leadership, they (and we at McKinsey) believed it was a trait invested in a single, powerful individual. Moreover, the many managers who should have been leading were too busy with their personal agendas, too busy serving on outside boards, or too involved in minutiae to have time to *do* what needed to be done. And those who tried to lead down the line were doing all the wrong things! It's a little late now, I realize, but I finally understand how we could have helped them be effective leaders.

At least there's no reason why you should repeat the mistakes of, among others, the Canadian lumber company, McKinsey, and Jim O'Toole. You can learn from the collective experience captured in these pages and then apply it to the work that needs to be done in your organization. (See the next entry, **Y**ou, the Leader.)

Y

LEADERSHIP
A to Z

You, the Leader

"What we need around here is some leadership." How often have you heard that plaintive lament? Chances are, you've said something like that yourself, and more than once. Typically, it is both true *and* the biggest cop-out since Theodore Kaczynski blamed his mother. To imply that leadership is someone else's responsibility—*their* responsibility up there, *anybody's* responsibility but yours—is to wiggle off the hook in the most wormlike fashion imaginable. In fact, for almost everyone in an organization, there is always an option to lead and the opportunity to do so—even if only one person reports to you. And if nobody reports to you, nothing is stopping you from leading your peers, your team, or your work group.

Of course, if you are not at the top of your organization, you don't have the benefit of the comforting list of excuses CEOs use when they choose to tread water rather than to lead. (See Why Leaders Won't Lead.) The best excuse available to folks down the line is that leadership isn't in your job description, and, thus, if you tried to lead, no one would follow. But, come on, there's nothing in your job description that *precludes* you from leading—and how do you know others won't follow if you haven't tried to lead?

"I tried to lead once, but no one followed" is the common back-up defense. But leadership is not worth trying if done just once. Almost everybody fails the first time. The trick is to examine why you failed (entries A through X should give you some clues), and then try again—this time with the added benefit of experience. Chances are you'll be more successful the second time around. Even if you aren't successful, you'll at least have the satisfaction that comes from knowing you really tried. And that's a lot more rewarding than sitting around and complaining, "What we need around here is some leadership."

LEADERSHIP
A to Z

Zenith

The paramount accomplishment for a leader is to successfully create conditions that allow followers to fulfill their aspirations. However, it is seldom the case that followers will either recognize, or thank, their leaders for doing so. The highest reward for leaders, then, is the satisfaction that comes from *self-fulfillment,* as Lao-tzu understood twenty-six hundred years ago:

> A leader is best
> When people barely know that he exists,
> Not so good when people obey and acclaim him,
> Worst when they despise him.
> "Fail to honor people,
> They fail to honor you";
> But of a good leader, who talks little,

When his work is done, his aim fulfilled,
They will all say, "We did this ourselves."

For a leader, it doesn't get any better than that.

Memorandum from Warren Bennis

To: The Reader
From: Warren Bennis
Subject: Jim O'Toole

Sometime in early spring of 1973, I was sitting at the breakfast table reading *The New York Times*. Most of the front page was filled with news about the fidgety Viet Nam peace talks and some muted rumblings about a burglary at the Watergate. My eyes glazed over those two epochal events and were drawn farther down the page, just below the crease of the paper. The article that caught my attention was a fascinating story about the publication of a book entitled *Work in America* written by a young scholar, James O'Toole, and a team of his colleagues. The MIT Press, it was reported, published it in record time, a famously scant thirty days, an astonishing accomplishment by any academic press. I learned that the study had been commissioned by the Department of Health, Education and Welfare. I'd never heard of O'Toole, but I was fascinated with the book's sweeping title about a topic close to my heart. So I hurried to the bookstore and finished reading it that morning.

Two things became clear to me about the book. First, it more than lived up to its title. Quite simply, it was the single best work I'd read about the current state of organizational behavior, experimental patterns of union-management relations, and leading change in corporate America. I loved O'Toole's style: fresh, adventurous, encompassing, but also clear, clean, and brisk. What a pleasure to read. No stale truths, no hackneyed, academic, off-putting jargon that social scientists, especially, seem to thrive on and are plagued by. W. H. Auden captured that well in his poem "Thou Shalt Not Commit a Social Science."

But it wasn't the style alone that intrigued me. It was O'Toole's thesis, his point of view. His was an elegant and powerful vision of work in the United States. He argued that the future of "good work" would depend on a participative, energized, and empowered workforce. Nowadays that thesis is so generally accepted (still more espoused than acted on) that it's become conventional wisdom and the butt of Scott Adams's cynical cartoons. Keep in mind that up to that point—it's 1973, don't forget—you could count on the fingers of one hand the writers who viewed the *corporation as a human community built on trust and respect for the worker and not simply a profit-making machine.* A rather lonely handful at that: Peter Drucker, Douglas McGregor, Chester Barnard, and Bob Townsend, all working at an angle to received truth, all restless iconoclasts, all advance scouts who could talk themselves and others into useful trouble. I figured O'Toole would soon join that group.

The book made history in more ways than I suspect its author could ever have imagined. A *Times* editorial was so rhapsodic that the book was elevated to a level rarely reached by an academic study. It fairly burst on the intellectual landscape, and suddenly *Work in America* became the most talked about book in intellectual and political circles. Lester Thurow reviewed it with relish (and with predictably mixed reaction; there wasn't enough economic analysis) in the lead article in the *New York Review of Books*. Conservative critic Irving Kristol weighed in for the *Wall Street Journal* and proceeded to savage it as dangerous neo-Marxist, agitprop nonsense. (This, despite the fact that the report had been endorsed strongly by HEW Secretary Elliot Richardson.) The liberal left didn't much care for it either. In fact, they were bitterly opposed to what they considered to be O'Toole's advocacy of "management Machiavellianism," which would arrogate the raison d'être of the union movement. And what do you know, they were right. They quite correctly (and haplessly) missed the point. Management did steal their thunder with serious results for the union movement that are only now being addressed. By the way, the book is still in print and has sold 120,000 copies. I should be so controversial!

The second thing that became clear to me that morning was that I wanted to meet the author. I didn't hesitate; I immediately phoned and implored him to take the next available plane and come talk to my top management team at the University of Cincinnati. He was game and took the red-eye that night. I met him at the airport the next morning and was taken aback by his appearance. This couldn't be my Jim O'Toole. He looked twenty-five, if that. He was a kid. How could he write that stuff at his age? What is he, I thought, an imposter or, worse, a precocious wunderkind? He was also bigger than I imagined him to be, *very* big, with an athlete's loping stride. He had a reposeful tilt to his body and distinctive walk that reminded me of Bill Bradley when he was playing for the Knicks and who, it turns out, was at Oxford and a fellow Rhodes Scholar the first year O'Toole was there (as was the other Bill during O'Toole's last year—but let's not go there). O'Toole didn't fit my stereotype of an Ivy Leaguer, either, which I had half suspected he would be, given his credentials as an Oxford D.Phil in social anthropology. A bit rumpled, casual, on the edge of disheveled, perhaps from his long, red-eyed trip.

But what I remember most from that first meeting in 1973 were his love affair with ideas, his impatience with the status quo, his passion about the "little murders" that he felt afflicted most contemporary organizations, his mind ranging wide from the politics of South Africa, which he had studied for his doctorate, to the latest Pinter play. Most of all, though, it was his questions that got me, his incessant questioning that excited me. He was the "great asker." That first meeting with Jim O'Toole was like popping the cork of your first bottle of champagne, effervescent and memorable, and to this day I recall it as a revivifying experience.

Later that year, Jim invited me to participate in a seminar at the Aspen Institute. In 1973–74, he was the director of the Institute's Program on Education, Work, and the Quality of Life, another happy indication of his book's influence. I had a house in Aspen back then and the thought of hanging out that summer with Jim and other friends was welcome and richly deserved, I felt, after a rather turbulent year at the University of Cincinnati. Another unexpected bonus was getting to know the O'Toole family: his extraordinarily gifted and attractive wife, Marilyn, and the two O'Toole colleens, Erin and Kerry. Working and playing with Jim was more fun than fun. So much learning, so much richness in this collaboration, and, given our intellectual affinities, which were broad enough to allow us to traverse a capacious landscape, our familiarity turned into a comfortable and close friendship. Someone, I forget who it was, said something about Franklin Roosevelt that reminded me of Jim. FDR, it was said, could make a casual visitor believe that nothing was as important to him that day as this particular visit and that he had been waiting all day for this hour to arrive. It was like that with the young Professor O'Toole.

Fast forward to April 1979. I was recovering from what my British doctors called a "moderately roughish" heart attack and was recuperating in improbable quarters, the flat of Charles and Elizabeth Handy, compressed into the wall of Henry the Third's wing of Windsor Castle. They had taken me in, so to speak, after I collapsed during a conference. The Handys graciously and generously looked over me for three long months as I wobbled back to health. Charles's books, as most readers of this book already know, have been an inspiration and a fount of ideas for many of us (and, coincidentally, he and Elizabeth have become close friends of the O'Tooles). A more important, almost Dickensian, coincidence occurred during my convalescence at Windsor. Jim O'Toole called, out of the blue, and invited me to join him on the faculty at the University of Southern California. It was a godsend. I was out of work. Literally. I was considering a number of professorships, but they all paled in comparison with going west and working with Jim, Larry Greiner, Ed Lawler, Steve Kerr, Ian Mitroff, and the all-star cast being assembled by the business school dean, Jack Steele, an intellectual outlaw who broke all the rules of the game and built the best management department in the world. I thought, oh yes, oh yes, here was a chance to really make a dent in the universe and make some useful mischief!

We did make a lot of useful mischief as we worked together over the next thirteen years. We started a magazine—Jim's brainchild, *New Management*— a precursor to the currently successful *FastCompany*. Because of its innovative design and readable style and appeal, some stodgy academics, undoubtedly threatened by the 'zine's uniformly high quality of writing and relevance, lobbied to cut off the funds. So we decided to invent something that wouldn't become so popular that our colleagues would want to destroy it: we cofounded the Leadership Institute in 1991, and it's still going, on the bootless chase for money, but with a promising future. Indeed, Jim has been inordinately good at creating organizations that are relevant and that last. While an undergraduate at USC, he and a fellow sophomore had organized a tutorial program for underprivileged high school kids in Watts—and put three hundred USC students to meaningful work in the ghetto right after the terrible summer of riots in 1965.

Now, I want to tell you some things that are in his formal resume. After finishing his preparatory studies at Oxford, Jim and Marilyn went to Cape Town, where he completed the field work for his dissertation, in which he compared the racial situation he knew so well in the United States to that in apartheid-era South Africa. During this time, he wrote periodically for *Time* and, as he says, "served time" at McKinsey. He then avoided getting into trouble while holding a low-level position in the Nixon administration and, from there, went to the Aspen Institute before settling down at USC for twenty years as the University Associates' Professor. Along the way, he wrote some thirteen books, including *Vanguard Management,* which was named "one of the best business books of 1985" by the editors of *Business Week.* His 1995 book, *Leading Change,* is arguably the best book on the topic. And did I mention that Jim was a protégé of the philosopher Mortimer Adler, serving under the master on the prestigious board of the *Encyclopaedia Britannica?* (Jim even wrote a book on political philosophy, *The Executive's Compass,* in his spare time.) Somehow, he also has managed to head the seminar programs at the Aspen Institute and direct the Booz·Allen & Hamilton Strategic Leadership Center (he currently chairs the academic Board of Advisors of that institution). Jim has now come full circle and has joined Ed Lawler's Center for Effective Organizations at USC as research professor.

When I recently asked Jim what, of all of the above, he considered to be the most important role he has played, he surprised me a bit when he unhesitatingly answered "teacher." Then I recalled that he was the only USC professor regularly to get a perfect 5 out of a possible 5 in his student evaluations. And his seminars at Aspen were always standing-room affairs. He is as good as they get. The "great asker."

A character in a John Irving novel repeatedly says, "I want to be of use." I think that describes Jim O'Toole's motivations best, to be of use. As you can tell from this book, a great inspiration in his life was Bob Townsend, who lived by the motto "No bullshit and treat people with respect." Pretty good rules, which Jim tries to follow. Over the quarter century I've known him, he's gone from wunderkind to wonderperson.

Acknowledgments

Like leading, writing is never a solo act. Here's a list of just a few of the many "coauthors" of this book.

The main participants in this effort were the partners of the distinguished consulting firm of Booz·Allen & Hamilton, whom I've had the enormous honor and pleasure of working with over the last half dozen years. I tried out all the stuff in these pages on them—and they tried out an equal amount of their new intellectual capital on me—in a mutual process of show and tell, give and take, and criticize and revise. I've benefited greatly from this relationship. What scholar wouldn't want the support of a practical "lab" in which to try out ideas on the world's brainiest professionals? I really should list the names of all 250 Booz·Allen partners here, but there are two, in particular, to whom I owe an unrepayable debt of gratitude for their friendship, mentoring, support, wisdom, and leadership: Paul Anderson and Bruce Pasternack are on my international first team of consulting all-stars. In addition, I offer my admiration and thanks to their partners Gary Ahlquist, Chuck Allison, Cyrus Friedheim, Shelley Keller, Dan Lewis, Gary Neilson, Ralph Shrader, and Tom Williams.

But, please note, none of the above shoulder any responsibility for whatever misuses I may have made of their work or for the outlandish opinions I felt compelled to vent. (I confess to ignoring their wise counsel to start behaving more maturely given my advancing age.)

I also have a marvelous support group of noted scholars whose research, theories, and insights have greatly informed the contents of this book. All hail Keith Berwick, Joanne Ciulla, Tom Cronin, Sumantra Ghoshal, Charles Handy, Ron Heifetz, Ed Lawler, and Tom Peters (a great gentleman who is, also, a true scholar). And George Thibault was my go-to source on everything from Shakespeare to military leadership.

From the world of practice, I've appropriated a passel of practical knowledge by observing the brilliant leadership of Skip Battle, John Biggs, Bob Davids, Max DePree, Kevin Fickenscher, David Law-Smith, Jay Marshall, Alan Mullaly, Bill Stasior, George Tenet, Pete Thigpen, Joe Thompson, Thom Thompson, and David Young.

Books require technical support, as well, and for that I must thank the highly skilled Jossey-Bass team, whose talents were complemented on this book by the contributions of acclaimed detective novelist Catherine Dain.

And to my old friend, teacher, and colleague Warren Bennis, thanks to you I don't feel bad about the prospect of not reading my own obituary!

Finally, Joan Townsend knows who deserves the most thanks for his contributions to this book.

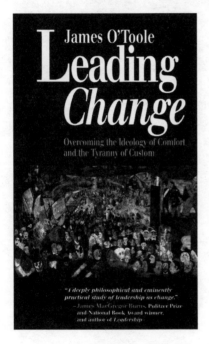
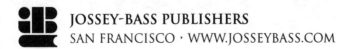